WEST VANCOUVER STORIES

THE WELLNESS EDITION

Edited by LINDY PFEIL

"The world is full of magic things,
patiently waiting for our senses to grow sharper."

W.B. Yeats

About The Wellness Edition

This is the third book in the *West Vancouver Stories* series. Over the course of three weeks, 25 writers (aged 11 to 87), gathered at the West Vancouver Memorial Library to share stories that explore wellness in all its dimensions – physical, mental, emotional, and spiritual.

A 2022 Angus Reid Institute study underscores the vital role of belonging in wellbeing, revealing that Canadians with a strong sense of connection report significantly higher life satisfaction. This anthology embodies that idea, serving as both an archive and a testament to the power of shared experience to bridge divides and build a more connected future.

The stories in this collection speak of resilience, courage, and creativity. They highlight the transformative power of community and the importance of truly listening to one another – of finding stillness amidst the noise. They celebrate the North Shore's spectacular beauty and rich cultural life, reminding us that wellness lies in nurturing what uplifts and brings us joy.

These accounts of rediscovering passions, overcoming challenges, and forging meaningful connections reveal that our collective wellbeing begins with the simple act of sharing our lives. Our health, our environment, and our relationships are deeply intertwined.

Storytelling has long been a powerful medium for building community. It creates spaces where individuals can share experiences, foster empathy, and transform isolated 'I's into a collective 'we.'

Within these pages, may you find reflections of your own life, discover moments of inspiration and connection, and be reminded that wellness is not just an individual pursuit, but a communal journey.

Lindy Pfeil
2025

with gratitude to …

◊ West Vancouver Foundation for partially funding this project with a Neighbourhood Small Grant

◊ West Vancouver Memorial Library for providing the location for our writing sessions and our book launch, and for being so welcoming to all

◊ the Coast Salish peoples, on whose unceded lands we live and write

◊ the writers who supported one other with such kindness during the writing and editing process

◊ the "characters" in these pages, some of whom may never know they have been immortalised

◊ Syeda Erum Noor for so generously sharing her talent and energy in gifting us our spectacular cover

◊ everyone who reads these stories

Stories

EXERCISE

Anne Baird

When I was five, during World War II, my family lived in Mourne Diablo, Trinidad – a remote oil company site. My father, a petroleum engineer for Trinidad Leaseholds, was tasked with developing offshore oilfields for the Allied war effort. He didn't just plan from behind a desk; he shimmied up oil derricks and worked alongside his crew.

Few expats lived there. My big brother, Bill, was away at boarding school. My little brother, Jim, was a baby. I had nobody to play with!

I spent my days running through the forest, sneaking down to the beach to spy on the steel bands, and climbing the mango tree where Bill had built me a platform "office." There, I drew, wrote stories, and communicated with the birds, monkeys, and wild donkeys who were my daily companions. Exercise was *living*. My community? The world of nature.

Back then, daily life provided exercise for everyone. Farmers planted, tended and harvested crops. Miners tackled seams of coal deep underground with pickaxes and shovels. Fishermen cast nets and hauled in their barrels of fish. Then they carted them home, hawking them through streets in creels and heavy baskets.

Women swept floors, beat rugs, cooked, scrubbed, and hung laundry on sagging lines. They gave birth, suckled babies, fed large families, planted gardens, tended the sick, and cared for animals. Children, once old enough, toiled alongside their parents, often following them into the family line of work.

After a day of labour like that, who needed yoga or hip-hop classes? A pint at the pub or relaxing by the fire was reward enough. Community thrived in workplaces, trade guilds, churches, and homes.

Then came the Industrial Revolution. Starting in the 1700s, it brought machines that eased much of the drudgery of earlier times. Farmers, miners, and labourers gradually gained access to tools that lightened their load. Women benefitted too, with devices like washing machines, vacuum cleaners, freezers, and prepared foods freeing them to try new activities – even work outside the home!

This era of modernization lessened the need for physical labour to survive. People lived longer and had more energy to innovate and increase productivity.

Factories and group enterprises sprang up, offering salaries and social benefits. Work became less about brawn and more about brainpower.

But there were losses. Factory assembly lines turned workers into cogs in a soulless machine, stripping the pride and variety of personal craftsmanship. Work no longer guaranteed the exercise or personal satisfaction of earlier generations.

With work-related exercise declining, people turned to walking, sports, and other activities to stay fit – if they weren't too exhausted after a day in the factory. Community, though still centered on family and work, expanded to include leisure and shared interests.

Now, in the digital age, computers, the internet, mobile phones, and AI have transformed our world beyond the wildest dreams of our ancestors. Many jobs require little physical effort. Sitting alone at desks or in home offices, people tap away at keyboards, connecting through emails and social media rather than face-to-face. Muscles go unused, and minds often feel disconnected. Our physical interactions with others have been diminished.

The result? Loneliness and isolation, unprecedented in 2025. To keep healthy, practice social skills and meet other human beings, exercise is more important than ever.

I experienced this when I immigrated to Canada in 1997. Moving to West Vancouver, where my parents had lived for 30 years, I found my brother Jim and his family welcoming but busy. I had to find my own way.

I moved into a tiny apartment near the community center and joined Jim's once-a-week exercise group at the old Masonic Hall on Bellevue Avenue. This was my first exercise group since leaving Bishop Strachan School in Toronto in 1949. There, climbing ropes, leaping over gym horses, and wobbling across balance beams had soured me on exercise. But Jim's gentle group of seniors running slow laps around the gym changed my perspective. They became my first Canadian friends.

I didn't stop there. I joined the community centre's workout programs. Aquafit classes on Mondays and Fridays, gym workouts on other days – it all became a vital part of my routine. In these classes, I found my forever friends.

Exercise not only brought me community; it saved me from knee replacement surgery. After a nasty fall, I was scheduled for surgery, but during a pre-op examination nine months later, the nurse was surprised.

"Why are you having surgery?" she asked. "You're in the top 90th percentile of patients I examine. You don't need it! What have you been doing?"

"Exercise," I replied.

"Well, whatever you're doing, keep it up!"

And I did.

THE GOLD DRESS

Anne Labelle

It's a vivid memory, infused with strong emotions; however, I'm not sure whether my recollection of the facts is entirely accurate. Over decades of tellings and retellings – by me, my siblings, and my parents – the story may have shifted slightly from reality. Still, it holds truth.

I was five years old, wearing church clothes and sock feet, fresh from Midnight Mass. We had come home to open presents, as we always did. It was officially Christmas morning, even though it was still night outside. The large bay window framed a scene of falling snow, sparkling under the warm glow of our home.

In the living room stood the tree, decorated with coloured lights and ornaments, and topped with an angel.

It was enormous, stretching to the ceiling, dominating the small room already crowded with my family of nine.

Under the tree, a few boxes wrapped in colourful paper (with no bows) lay on the wooden floor. I can still feel the warmth of the floor, regularly polished by my mother with an ancient green metal machine which my father had likely scavenged – a relic of his thriftiness as a child of the Great Depression and a naval veteran of World War II.

There was a real fireplace, brick painted white, with a dark wood mantle – or maybe the mantle was painted white, too. There was no fire, because of the tree.

Hanging on the mantle was my Christmas present: the Gold Dress – the gift I had wished for months earlier.

Sometime in October or November, my parents had asked about my Christmas wish. I wanted only one thing: a golden dress made entirely of sunshine. To my young mind, this golden dress was far more magical than the two others mentioned in my favourite story at the time – a silver dress made of moonbeams and one of starlight. I don't remember the story anymore, only the three dresses. Or maybe there were only two – sunshine and moonbeams – and I added the starlight later because in fairytales things often come in threes.

Although made from the finest gold, the dress was simple, and appropriate for my age and diminutive frame. A-line, falling from the shoulders with a rounded neckline, no collar, a short zipper up the back, and slim ¾-length sleeves. And it was gold!

The fabric was pure 1960s – a flashy check pattern of ½-inch squares of sparkly gold lamé alternating with squares embroidered in shiny gold thread. The contrast was mesmerizing. Matching slippers, made from fabric scraps, completed the outfit.

I put it on immediately and wore it constantly until it was threadbare – even while playing in the street the following spring and summer, as children back then could safely do.

In those days, my mother made all our clothes, except for the ones donated by the church. Dark green plastic bags of cast-offs and high fashion arrived in our apartment from time to time. Once, I chose a small dress for my doll but was persuaded by my father to return it for another child who might need it more.

In my young imagination, my mother searched far and wide for this rare fabric – a heroic and possibly impossible quest – to fulfil her youngest child's singular Christmas wish.

Recently, I asked my sister, six years my senior, what she remembered.

"Oh, we all got clothes for Christmas that year," she said. A yellow dress for her, a plaid vest for our eight-year-old brother, socks for the four older ones, who were all adults in their 20s by this point. "Mom just went to Kresge's for your fabric." Kresge's was a discount clothing and household goods store in Montreal, where we lived in the 1960s. "Also, we went to mass in the afternoon on Christmas Eve, so it wasn't night outside."

Another shock. Daytime. And only the three youngest children were home for Christmas that year.

I didn't ask about the falling snow sparkling outside the bay window, in case that wasn't real either.

Mostly, the story of the gold dress is about a mother's great effort to bring joy to her child with limited resources.

For me, it's a tale of pure love, one I prefer to remember as a fairytale, even if it's viewed through gold-coloured glasses.

LIFTING EACH OTHER UP
Chén'chenstway

Brenda Morrison

A story in three parts, held by the curve of time and grounded in the strength of mountains.

I love mountains.

I was raised on the slopes of Vancouver's North Shore Mountains. Following in my father's footsteps, I hiked through the crisp forest air, past West Lake and Hollyburn Lodge. My imagination carried me on endless adventures, exploring mountains that seemed to cascade forever up the coast from Vancouver.

I was raised in the British Properties by the broth of Scots who had settled on these lands. In school, we recited the Lord's Prayer every morning, sang "God Save the Queen," and raised the Canadian flag.

We paid a nickel to cross the newly built Lions Gate Bridge for picnics at Lumberman's Arch in Stanley Park, gazing back at the two peaks – The Lions – that crowned the mountains. These Lions were named after the Trafalgar Square lions in London, seat of the British Empire. I was raised by the stiff upper lip of rugged individualism that prides itself on conquering mountains.

I love mountains.

That love took me to Nepal in 1993 where the call of the Himalayas was irresistible. Hiking solo, I crossed a rugged glacier, traversed Chola Pass, and forded a mighty river toward Everest – the Queen of all mountains. At over 29,000 feet, Mount Everest stands six times taller than The Lions.

In Gorak Shep, the original Everest Base Camp, I arrived just as more than a hundred runners set off on the world's highest marathon to Namche Bazaar. They ran downhill the entire way – what a crazy bucket list feat! I descended at my own pace, travelling from teahouse to teahouse. I loved being alone on the trail, grounded by the mountains.

One morning, after staying overnight in a welcoming tea house, I slipped out early. I thought I had the trail to myself. Then I heard footsteps behind me. Each step mirrored mine. My body tightened, adrenaline flooding through me. Was I being followed? Every cell was on alert.

My mind raced with fear. For every step I took, the person behind me matched it. A ghostly stalker.

Listening deeply for clues, my body gradually relaxed. Perhaps I wasn't being followed. Perhaps I was being accompanied. We walked in rhythm for a few miles. When the footsteps quickened, my heart raced again. The man passed me, smiled, and kept walking. I smiled back, relieved. Later that day, as I passed through another village, we waved to each other like old friends.

I continued alone, passing village after village on my way to Jiri for the bus to Kathmandu. Each day, I inhaled the mountain air, enjoying the stillness of my mind and the simple hospitality of the Nepalese people. Toward the end of my journey, I joined a group of walkers for a day and stayed overnight at the same teahouse. The next morning, eager for solitude, I planned to walk alone again.

At the trailhead, a strange energy filled the village. People were buzzing with news. An uneasy feeling swept over me.

A man stepped out from the crowd.

"We do not want you to walk alone today," he said.

This was my last day on the trail. I was certainly going to walk it alone.

"We do not want you to walk alone today," he repeated.

I stared, confused.

"Someone has been assaulted on the trail," he explained. "We want you to walk with the group you were with yesterday."

Stunned, I fell silent. Who was this 'we?' How did they know about my solo journey? My worldview of rugged individualism collapsed, tumbling like a landslide into the valley below. I had never been walking alone. I had never been conquering mountains. Me, myself, and I became we, ourself, and us.

It was a humbling revelation. A lesson from the mountains and the people who call them home. That 'we' resonated across the valley, from teahouse to teahouse, echoing over the highest pass I had crossed.

There is a 'we' in wellness. Like safety, it is a collective responsibility. Across time and place, we hold a mutual responsibility for one another.

I love the mountains.

In 2006, I returned to the North Shore Mountains that raised me. My home is now Nex̱wlélex̱wm. I look across the Salish Sea to those peaks and continue to learn from the Sḵwx̱wú7mesh Úxwumixw (Squamish Nation), who have stewarded this land since time out of mind.

I grew up not far from the Capilano River, named after Chief Joe (S7ápelek) and Mary (Lixwelut) Capilano, leaders of Sḵwx̱wú7mesh Úxwumixw, who intimately knew the crags and crevices of the glacier-cut North Shore Mountains. Joe was the first person to scale the western peak of The Lions while hunting mountain goats. Mary's grandfather met Captain Vancouver when he first anchored on the shores of what would become known as Vancouver.

Joe and Mary Capilano tell the story of the Twin Sisters – Ch'ích'iyúy Elx̱wíḵn – a story far richer than Trafalgar Square's namesake lions. It is a tale that spans the ages.

During a time of war, a grand chief hosted a potlatch to celebrate his twin daughters coming of age. At their request, he invited his enemies to the celebration. The feast of abundance, gratitude, and reciprocity brought peace to the warring nations. The Creator, moved by the sisters' wisdom, immortalized their gesture of peace – to be held by the curve of time – by raising them as mountains for all to behold.

The arc of mountains transcends time. If you listen closely, you can hear the voice of the ancestors rising from the valleys, spilling over the peaks, whispering ancient wisdom to those whose ears are tuned to their vibration. Their song has held us since time out of mind.

A 'STICK TO IT' STORY

Bruce McArthur

The Pacific Coast offers many beaches to explore, and I enjoy spending time on them, looking for items that can be repurposed. These beaches reveal the interplay between the natural world and human-made or manipulated objects. The beaches and shoreline also highlight the cooperation that sustains our comfortable existence. Quiet moments by the shore allow me to delve into the unknown and imagine mysteries waiting to be solved. Beaches hold pieces of the past – some discarded waste, some lost treasures ripe for recycling, and some that can be transformed into representations of the present or visions of the future.

One of my favourite beaches surrounds Rebecca Spit on Quadra Island. Small, weathered pieces of cedar can be gathered and then shaped into recognizable forms. I've used these to soften the intrusive chain-link fence sections in my backyard. Hung on the fence are replicas I've crafted from my driftwood collections – crescent moon faces, round planet shapes, a large owl with outstretched wings, and the tail of a whale just visible above its submerged body. A large frog, crafted from these small pieces, welcomes visitors at our entrance. I often joke that if anyone reacts negatively to my driftwood creations, I'll create a huge dinosaur figure.

Another favourite beach is at Ambleside, where tidal gifts and the interaction between the animate and inanimate are a constant. For the past two years, I've been crafting walking sticks from branches that wash up on West Vancouver's shores. I search until I find three decent ones, then sit in a comfortable spot to shave them, cut them to appropriate lengths, and round the ends. During these meditative moments, I'm often interrupted by passersby who stop to watch or ask questions, by the parade of crab fishermen taking advantage of the fertile waters at Ambleside Pier, or by the sounds of panhandlers playing tunes and regulars conversing with strangers. The chugging trains, which can be heard from the nearby tracks, offer their squeal of wheels, the occasional horn blast, and the clang of bells where the railway crosses the road. Near the shore, eagles squawk while pigeons, crows, and seagulls announce their displeasure at their presence. Herons, geese, and ducks transition between the shore and the sea. On the water, swimmers, kayakers, sailboarders, yachts, freighters, ferries, and cruise ships create constant activity. Above, various planes fly by, adding their own sounds to the scene.

The water activity creates waves that pound the beach, while changing weather brings ripples to the shore, emphasizing the boundary between land and ocean. In the distance, the sun setting over Vancouver Island provides a unique glow, reminding me that the earth is just a small part of a greater whole.

While walking these beaches, I often find discarded and abandoned materials. Some are garbage, but others are surprises. Once, I came across the carcass of an octopus, giving me a rare chance to examine it closely. I've also found a long wooden-handled pike pole, a short rope with a loop and a monkey fist knot (which I imagine was used for casting a tie-up line), and many plastic floating toys that I recover and leave for others in the kids' water park area. The tides deliver logs and timber of various shapes and sizes, especially after rainstorms that raise the levels of the numerous creeks flowing into West Vancouver.

But my main focus is finding tree branches that can be shaped into walking sticks. Once cleaned and shaped, I leave them for others to enjoy. Over fifty have been completed, and only once did I find one returned to the ocean, then washed back up onto the shore.

These walking sticks not only recognize the bounty that the ocean delivers but also contribute to my imaginary connections with the past and future. I leave three finished sticks, shaped like the letter 'A,' on a large granite block at the head of Ambleside Pier. To me, this symbol subtly refers to my family name, McArthur, and evokes the legend of King Arthur, whose sword was embedded in a stone, its removal a blessing.

Strangers notice and take these sticks, and some magic or usefulness seems to occur for the new owners. I feel a warmth around the transformation of an item delivered by nature, evolving into something useful to humans, and perhaps even gaining a personality of its own.

DIVING INTO CHANGE

Chantal Cameron

The summer of 2024 brought a whirlwind of change.

One morning, a friend sent me a link to the women's 1-metre diving event at the Olympic Games. Grateful for the distraction, I clicked without hesitation, eager for a brief reprieve from the chaos in my mind.

My life had been flipped upside down. I wasn't just navigating changes – I was drowning in them. Layoffs had become the tech world's grim new normal, and one month before my wedding I found my name on that dreaded list. My only lifeline was the chance of securing another internal role, but the clock was ticking. Balancing wedding preparations with job applications and interviews felt impossible. Change was something I'd craved in the abstract, but not like this – not all at once, with this crushing weight.

Overwhelmed, I sought mental escapes. Wedding vendor calls, job applications, and interviews blurred into an exhausting loop. Every decision felt monumental, every option overwhelming. Social media doom-scrolling became my way of zoning out. The link to the diving event? Another fleeting escape, a way to disconnect from my spiralling thoughts, even if only for a moment.

Watching diving always takes me back to simpler times. Back then, my biggest challenges played out at the pool. Hours were spent between training sessions, my hair perpetually damp and tinged with the smell of chlorine.

I longed for the days when life was measured by a list of compulsory dives: front, back, reverse, inward, and twist.

The process of learning a new dive was methodical and almost ritualistic. It began with visualization – watching videos in slow motion, dissecting every movement, and mentally walking through every step until it felt ingrained. Then came the trampoline, where deliberate over-rotation helped internalize the mechanics. Finally, it was time to face the real thing, standing on the edge of the board, heart racing.

Most dives didn't land cleanly on the first or even the second attempt. But the moment everything clicked was transformative. Success wasn't just visible; it was visceral. In that flow state, the dive in your mind aligned perfectly with reality, offering a fleeting sense of freedom. That was the nirvana of diving. That feeling lingered long after I left the pool.

Each dive had a difficulty factor. Some I mastered, while others left me paralyzed with fear. The reverse dive was my nemesis. Facing forward but launching backward felt unnatural, like defying gravity in the worst way. Twice during practice, I miscalculated, and my face slammed into the board. The sting of failure lasted far longer than the physical pain. That dive became my mental roadblock. Before every competition, my stomach twisted into knots, dreading the moment I'd have to step on the board and face it.

Diving is as much about mental clarity as physical skill. Overthink, and you're doomed.

My coach always said: "You're a better diver when you turn your brain off."

Easy to say. Hard to do. Standing on the edge of the board, my mind replayed every worst-case scenario. Often, my fears became reality.

That's exactly how I felt now – trapped in the same cycle of fear and hesitation. Years of hard work, late nights, and professional wins had culminated in a layoff. Just like that. A one-month deadline loomed with no clear path ahead. Taking the leap felt impossible, yet staying in limbo felt equally unbearable. I kept waiting for clarity, for courage. But time doesn't wait, and neither did the mounting pressure.

A memory surfaced, unbidden but welcome. During a competition at a new pool, I had misjudged a jump in warm-ups and rocketed to the bottom, spraining my ankle on impact. My coach patched me up, and I nearly called it quits. At the last minute, I decided to compete anyway. What did I have to lose? I figured I'd bomb, but at least the trip wouldn't be completely wasted. With no expectations, I found my rhythm. Dive after dive, I nailed my execution, scoring higher than ever before. I ended up winning. My coach said it was the best I'd ever performed.

Why now? Why this memory? Diving taught me lessons I never expected to carry into adulthood. Sports teach teamwork, discipline, and resilience, but the deeper lessons sneak up on you. I learned that staying trapped in my own head is the surest way to fail. Fear of failure paralyzes. Letting it dictate my moves meant I had lost before I'd even begun.

Standing at this crossroads, I realized I was still that girl on the diving board, staring down the edge, heart pounding. The stakes were different, but the fear was the same. Moving forward required trust – trust in the leap, even without knowing where it would take me. I might stumble, even crash spectacularly. But I'd also remind myself what success felt like, and that made the leap worth it.

For now, it was one step at a time. One dive at a time.

FINDING JOY BEYOND APPLAUSE

Daina Zhu

Last spring, my daughters, Kate and Anne, eagerly participated in the North Shore Music Festival. Held in a small, cosy church in the heart of our community, the festival celebrated young talent and hard work. Participants were ranked by skill level, with the top performers receiving personalized trophies engraved with their names – cherished mementos of their dedication and artistry.

Kate and her friend Esther performed an electrifying rendition of Rimsky-Korsakov's "Flight of the Bumblebee." Their synchronized performance dazzled the judges, earning them a shared trophy. Anne, despite her diligent preparation and passion for music, struggled under the pressure of the competition. She faltered, making more mistakes than usual, and came home empty-handed, her confidence shaken. Anne has always been the more spirited and self-assured of my children, and seeing her so downcast, especially after all her hard work, broke my heart.

Several weeks later, on a sunny Friday evening, the festival organizers hosted a concert for the trophy recipients. The event showcased the award-winning performances and included the official trophy presentation. As a parent, I faced a dilemma. Should I focus on celebrating Kate's success, reveling in the applause and vanity of a proud parent? Or should I tend to Anne's wounded spirit, guiding her away from what felt like failure in her young eyes?

I chose the latter.

Instead of attending the concert, I took Anne and her younger brother, William, to a pottery workshop in West Vancouver. This community, with its stunning landscapes and welcoming atmosphere, is a haven of activities that nurture the soul. While Kate and Esther attended the concert, I explained to Anne why we were embarking on this different adventure. I wanted her to understand that life is about more than winning trophies – it's about finding joy and self-expression in unexpected places.

The pottery workshop proved to be the perfect choice. Nestled in a bright, airy studio with views of the mountains and ocean, the space radiated calm. The instructor greeted us warmly, and soon Anne and William were absorbed in shaping clay with their hands. The cool, pliable clay transformed under their touch, mirroring the magic of creativity.

Little William giggled as he experimented, his carefree joy filling the studio with laughter. As Anne focused on crafting a small, beautiful cup, her sadness melted away. By the end of the session, she proudly declared it a Mother's Day gift for me.

Surrounded by their happiness, I felt an overwhelming sense of gratitude – not just for the pottery class but for the nurturing spirit of West Vancouver. It reminded me why I love this community so much. More than a picturesque place, it's where the pressures of life soften, and the simple pleasures of creativity and connection come to the forefront. Whether you're a child shaping clay for the first time or an adult seeking peace in the rhythms of nature, this community has a way of nurturing the soul, of providing healing, belonging, and renewal.

Returning home that evening, I reflected on the day's choices. Some might argue that skipping the award ceremony deprived Anne of a valuable lesson in resilience. But I believe there will be plenty of opportunities for her to learn from challenges. For now, while her heart is tender, I want her to know that her worth isn't defined by trophies or applause. What matters is the effort she puts into her passions and the joy she discovers along the way.

Kate returned from the concert beaming with pride, clutching her trophy. She shared stories of the performances, her joy infectious. Anne listened with genuine interest, no longer burdened by inadequacy. In her hands, she held the small cup she had made – a treasure she was equally proud of. That evening, the four of us sat together, laughing, sharing stories, and admiring Anne's pottery. None of us could stop smiling.

West Vancouver played a pivotal role in transforming what could have been a day of disappointment into one of healing and joy. Life's most meaningful moments aren't always about winning. Sometimes, they're about discovering the beauty of the journey, finding strength in creativity, and embracing the comfort of a place that feels like home.

In the end, one child brought home a trophy, another brought home a handmade gift, and I brought home a priceless memory. This community, with its ability to inspire and uplift, gave us more than we ever expected. It gave us exactly what we needed.

The next day, I noticed a note stuck to Anne's piano. It was a list of tips for performing successfully at a piano competition, thoughtfully written by Kate. At the top of the list, one line stood out in bold: "Go to a clay workshop and bring back a light heart."

A LOVE LETTER TO AMBLESIDE

Debra Dolan

It happened so quickly. One moment I was reading at the back of the bus; the next, my life was forever altered. Nine years later, I still don't remember the jarring blow to my head when the TransLink driver slammed on the brakes to avoid a collision with a truck.

Then began the slow unraveling of an energetic life filled with activities, work, and people. Piece by piece, something or someone vanished until my days were spent recovering from one workday to the next. Evenings and weekends were spent in seclusion, marked by injury-related limitations. I hid my diminished abilities and raw emotions, sinking into the darker side of solitude. When I could no longer work or drive, I had to surrender fully to the reality that my life's trajectory had changed.

It felt like endless jet-lag – the best way I can describe living with a complicated head injury and post-concussion syndrome. Thoughts refused to connect with words, and my mind and body felt disconnected from each other and the world. Exhaustion ached through me.

Years passed with little relief. The constant pain heightened my irritability and strained my central nervous system. Coping became a full-time job. I never imagined this journey would take so much or last so long.

Rehabilitation forced me to leave home daily. I dreaded the prospect of encountering someone I knew, enduring unsolicited advice, or responding with a polite "Fine, thank you," to the ubiquitous "How are you?" Venturing into public required energy and careful planning, leaving me depleted. Even those with the best intentions couldn't truly understand. How could they? When I looked in the mirror, I didn't see it either.

I am deeply grateful that my injuries didn't rob me of life-long passions: writing, reading, walking, and connecting with friends and loved ones. Words come slower; books take longer to read and recall; invigorating walks around Stanley Park and global adventures are behind me. I am unlikely to return to the social life I once took for granted. Still, I persist. These simple acts have always saved me, teaching me more about myself than any lover, therapist, or the passage of time.

As the years progressed, I focused on what I could control and change to support my situation. Resting my brain allowed me to think more clearly. Surrounded by friends, a loving partner, and dedicated medical practitioners, I pursued wellness vigorously. Acceptance became key. To begin anew, I needed to confront endings and acknowledge that my challenges would follow me everywhere.

The time had come to leave the noise, grit, and chaos of the city. It no longer served my needs, only aggravating my symptoms and requiring every ounce of deliberation and care. After years of denial, I finally accepted my disability – a label I resisted but could no longer ignore.

I thought carefully about where I would next live. I needed a quieter, more supportive environment, with easy access to public transportation.

I considered several places: Revelstoke, Nelson, Whistler, and Victoria. Then, while looking at old photographs, I remembered Ambleside, the commercial heart and creative hub of West Vancouver. I first fell in love with this walkable seaside community in 1979 while visiting my uncle and his partner. In 1984, during my wanderlust twenties, I sublet a studio at 15th and Esquimalt for six months, before settling in various lower mainland locations. The area's natural beauty, with a view of Grouse Mountain, and vibrant vibe held a special place in my heart.

Although my unexpected, unwelcome circumstances forced me into early retirement, returning to this charming enclave after nearly forty years has brought me joy. Moving from East Van to West Van in 2022 meant more than simply moving westward from one side of Vancouver to another (and not to be confused with the westside or west-end of the city). It marked a transition through Stanley Park, over Lions Gate Bridge, and into renewal. I moved to a different municipality, and after nearly 25 years as a condo owner on 'the Drive,' I feel more at home in Ambleside than anywhere else in my life.

Ambleside is a hidden gem of small-town charm, modest population, and independent neighbourhood shops. It is the best of two worlds, offering a perfect blend of suburban tranquility and urban accessibility. It is a true blessing to live in a community one does not need to vacation from. In my home, I enjoy views of both the sea and North Shore Mountains and am steps away from the Centennial Seawalk. These surroundings play a vital role in my mental and physical wellness. The universe seemed to align when I purchased my home in a mid-century modern building with friendly neighbours who demonstrate pride of ownership.

The move shook up my life in all the right ways. I stopped waiting for my pre-injury life to return and embraced a new reality. This acceptance propelled me forward, away from self-pity. While natural healing has occurred since 2015, Ambleside's location and offerings inspire a balanced, fulfilling life. As an independent woman navigating the early stages of old age, walkability and convenience are essential to my health. Strolling between Park Royal and Dundarave, I have everything I need, and more. As my world shrank, it also expanded in unexpected ways.

Wellness is both an individual and collective pursuit. We shape it through our choices, behaviours and lifestyles, but it is also deeply influenced by our physical, social, and cultural environment. I feel as though I have won the lottery, living in this postcard come to life.

TAKE A WALK ON THE SEAWALL

Evelyn (Stephens) Dawson

Would you like to take a walk on the seawall?
We'll start at my home under the Lions Gate Bridge
On the Capilano 5 First Nations Reserve
In the Capilano Mobile Home Park.
My home is small, like an apartment. But on the ground.

You should know that for some time
I've had a fantasy of retiring in Ambleside, West Vancouver
And I've ended up close to my dream – living just a mile away in a small home to the east.

Many days I walk past my dream home(s) – just for exercise
And for the glorious experience.
It starts on a pathway south of Park Royal – and goes like
this . . .

A green forest with trees adjoining overhead
Some lean at precarious angles – what's holding them up?
Small birds twitter
Over-zealous bikers whizz by
A salty breeze counters the heat.

Canada geese take their teenagers for a swim on the
Capilano River
How much longer will they stay in line?
Traffic buzzes white noise from Lions Gate Bridge,
A crossing from the North Shore to Stanley Park.
Watch out for scootered children recently released from
school!

At the mouth of the river, a line of fishermen standing in
hip waders
Drawn far out by the low tide
Hopeful lines in the water
Will they catch a salmon (or two)?

And then – the dog park. Many memories here.
Wide grass field to run on
Tails wagging amid doggie dissent,
Giant log laying by the water
The one I sat on to cry when my own dog died.

Now wide sandy beaches, this time for humans
Tastefully lined with selected logs that wash up
Decorated with trendy rooty stumps
(Haven't we all seen that massive, uprooted tree in Stanley
Park?)
Miniature copies of the gigantic sculpture at Grosvenor
Place.

White noise of skateboarders in the park
Large ocean liners hoot at smaller craft to get out of the
way
(What are these smaller craft thinking?)
Huge container ships precariously piled with cargo
Comically appear taller than the UBC headland.

A dozen neon green sails flutter away in the bay
Lesson craft from the marina
Vast expanse of blue water matches the blue sky,
Adeptly concealing Vancouver Island with haze.
Only the height of her mountains is revealed,
Demarcated by a row of fluffy clouds.

Multi-million-dollar project to raise a shoreside heritage
building
Surrounded by expertly-practised West Vancouver
landscaping
Beautiful flowers are sprinkled here and there, carefully
tended.
Next a community garden
And then the lot belonging to the latest house demolished

Replaced simply by grass
Awaiting release from fences
To be walked upon.

A path leads back to the beach
Here sprinkled with more rooty stumps
That reach wildly askew
In all directions
Fringed by fireweed, sumac, and wildflowers.

Tame crows entertain us – hoping for tossed food scraps
They know we have some.
Small children scale beached logs
A tipi fort made from driftwood
Is left standing for their use.

A small water park and structures alluding to a pirate ship,
Second or third generation structures,
They don't need a real ship – just a suggestion
My children played here. And thirty years since, a
grandchild too,
Toy seagulls joined on high by the real thing – comical.

A long swig from my water bottle – still cold from the ice
inside
It's hazy overhead today – a small respite from an unusually
warm summer.

Another heritage building – this one boarded up
Languishing from lack of funds,

Rustic bridge over the salmon-restored stream
And then open seawall – dog free and bicycle free – a rare treat for humans!

Bordered by luxury waterfront homes.
Single dwellings, duplexes, town homes, tall and small apartment buildings
Pretty much all financially out of my reach (yes, I'm envious)
But pleasant to walk beside. Who lives there? Where did they get their money?

Bumblebee-laden catnip beds. A soft violet colour.
Another fish-enabled creek. Some serious work on "fish passage,"

A sign warns of an "active CN Rail line"
Beside which dogs enter
To stay fenced off from the seawall
While their human owners enjoy its expanse
Who ever heard of such a thing?
Only in West Vancouver.

Sun-dried brown grass stands along the fence,
Smoke tree, butterfly bush, pine tree, roses, big leaf maple, blackberries
Green growth barricading the tracks
Broken by the occasional human crossing here or there
Forming a path between those homes and the seawall.

This year the blackberries are abundant
But no water to expand and ripen them
Dried bits produce seed but no flesh to attract
consumption.

At the end of the seawall a small, cosy village – Dundarave.
Sometimes I sit on the logs there and stare at the waves
In a reverie. My comforting place. Calming rhythms,
Smooth rocks remind me of my childhood
Sitting by those other smooth rocks in a farmyard driveway
Choosing my favourites…

A glorious yarn shop that fuels my knitting,
It used to be a second-hand store
Where I found my fused glass representation
Of the mountains surrounding Jasper, Alberta
Thank you, Ms. Roe.

Restaurants and Delany's where I lunch on occasion
Then the bus stop where I board to go back home
A three-mile walk is enough for me, and a $1.95 bus ride is
a bargain.
I travel again past my dream homes and try to decide which
one I'll live in
I am allowed to dream, aren't I?
My life is good in retirement, and I am forever grateful.
Thank you for accompanying me today on my walk.

*Postscript: Dogs are now allowed on the seawall on leashes. The yarn
store has been demovicted.*

NOT AS EASY AS IT SEEMS

Hestia Li Ang

Have you heard of Odysseus? In Greek mythology, he's known for his cunning, wit, and cleverness. He was the one who came up with the Trojan Horse idea. Then he spent 20 years trying to return home after the war, encountering many hardships along the way.

Meanwhile, his wife, Penelope, was being harassed by a group of suitors who believed Odysseus was dead and wanted to marry her. Odysseus was the king of Ithaca and so the suitors wanted to claim his throne. But they faced an obstacle: Telemachus, the rightful heir to the throne. As the only son of Odysseus and Penelope, the kingship would automatically fall to him on his twentieth birthday. So, the suitors planned on killing him before then. They intended to ambush him as he returned from his search for his father.

I would *not* cope with being the prince in that situation. It would be terrifying. While Odysseus eventually returned home and killed the suitors, in the real world, there isn't always justice.

Killing for power or wealth is never justified. Yet blackmail, threats, and violence are disturbingly common nowadays. Even something as ordinary as walking down the street can be risky. Tragedy can strike in unimaginable ways.

Take 9/11, for example – an unspeakable crime that violated the trust we put in one another. Does this mean that everyone you meet is dangerous? Probably not. But cracks in civilization allow chaos and disorder to seep through.

In Egyptian mythology, Apophis, a serpent, personified chaos. The Egyptians called chaos itself Isfet. Ma'at, on the other hand, embodied order and harmony.

Although my family and I haven't experienced terrible crimes, I know happy endings aren't guaranteed. Recovering from suffering isn't easy, and it usually changes people drastically.

One lesson I have learned at school is this: "The past is everything we were; it's not who we are." This idea is often tied to forgiveness – understanding that people can change and giving them the benefit of the doubt. It encourages hope for the best instead of suspicion and assuming the worst. But it also raises a question: How far can someone go before change is no longer possible?

Even if a person shows remorse, it doesn't erase the pain others endured during their recovery. Maybe the perpetrator needed help. Maybe, with enough support, the tragedy could have been avoided.

But "maybe" doesn't undo the harm. Or make things right.

The past is everything that shaped us and brought us here. But it doesn't define us. Small actions can ripple into massive consequences. Rather than helping someone recover, we should try to prevent the tragedy from happening in the first place. Many people grow up in tough circumstances. We don't get to choose our families or our starting points. But we can start where we are, use what we have, and do what we can in life, remembering that one small match can create a huge explosion.

HOWE SOUND HOME

Inga Pedersen McLaughlin

I savour my quiet moments in my happy place – the garden. At peace with my thoughts, I methodically pull endless weeds and encroaching ivy, finding time to breathe, think, and process an often-chaotic life. How fortunate to live overlooking beautiful Howe Sound. Many of us call this place home, including numerous birds and animals – even bears, eagles, and whales.

Our bird-friendly village has bylaws to protect our feathered friends, prohibiting tree trimming during nesting season. It's remarkable how tiny a hummingbird nest can be. Even outside nesting season, I worry about trimming the front hedge. What if there's a home hidden within?

My knowledgeable neighbour, a true hummingbird whisperer, once advised me: "Just pay attention. If there's a hummingbird nest, they'll let you know."

Wise words. I started to listen more. Listen to the wildlife.

Inhale. Mmm… pine trees and ocean air.

Chirp!

"Hello, Red," I say, as he flutters onto the rock wall and hops along behind me. "Sorry about the noisy leaf blower yesterday."

He freezes, cocks his head sideways, as if to say, "Watcha doin'?" He sneaks bravely closer as I pull weeds, then plunges headfirst into some freshly turned dirt, proudly surfacing with a wriggling worm. Not my ideal breakfast, but I'm glad he's happy. No judgement here. I glance at the patch of tiny wild strawberries – just fingernail size – so sweet and much better than store-bought.

"Those make a good breakfast. I was leaving them for you."

Chirp.

"But if you aren't going to eat them, I bet Squizz will."

He nods as if he understands and flutters off to his home in the maple tree. It's made of moss far softer than the twig Robin's nests I've seen in bird books – I think he's a bit of an overachiever.

I wonder if Squizz is around. The little Western squirrel who lives in the cedar tree has been scurrying about all day, searching and gathering. His morning routine includes climbing high into the fir trees and methodically dropping pinecones onto our roof. We often wake to the rhythmic thuds, like an alarm clock telling us to get up. Squizz then spends the rest of the day retrieving his treasures one by one and carting them back up to his home in the cedar tree.

Squizz and I have a special relationship with an unspoken rule: "I don't go in your tree, and you don't come in my house."

He enjoys following me around the garden as I plant bulbs – he digs them up. It's a love-hate thing, but I don't mind. He pretends he doesn't see where I plant them, or maybe he forgets. Either way, he chirps ecstatically when he digs up a "surprise" bulb. Always keeping a keen ear out for bears, his hearing is much better than mine and he's the first to freeze, chirp, and skedaddle at the telltale snap of twigs.

The bears prefer the shortcut through our backyard to the creek, but I don't mind although I cherish my time outside. When the bears want to be in the garden, I feel I should not be there. Squizz and the birds are good alarms; the birds always know what's going on before anyone else, their flurry of tweets and chirps alerting me to intruders. But we all know that the garden is a shared space, where all are welcome and expected to get along.

Squawk!

Tardy and not to be left out, Blue, a scrawny Steller's jay, haphazardly clatters onto the chimney, feathers askew as if he woke in a hurry. He hops efficiently across the roof, tossing leaves from the gutter, earning his keep with his obsessive cleanup. His usual morning greeting involves hanging upside down from the eaves, peering through the window to check if we're awake. Today he's running late.

Somebody in the neighbourhood must be feeding him peanuts, as he seems to have a solid stash. He saves them for a rainy day, burying them deep in my planters, often returning to frantically search for them, with an "I'm sure I put them here" expression on his face. He looks baffled when he comes up with only pathetic mouthfuls of dirt. I haven't the heart to tell him his peanuts have gone to the Land of Squizz,

Ah, it's golden hour already! I've been so lost in my thoughts I almost missed the sunset. I love sunsets – colourful blessings to share with loved ones. It's my favourite time of day, always different yet always the same, dependable. I set aside my pruners and head to the deck as light bounces off the cedar beams, filling our home with warmth. The animals make their way home too. I'm alone today; everyone in my human family is out of town. My youngest sent a photo of the sunset from her Brooklyn, New York rooftop.

Outside, I watch the clouds turn breathtaking colours of gold, then slowly become every imaginable shade of pink, soft and gentle as they reflect on the mirror-like sea. Strikingly fluorescent as the sun dips closer to the islands, it's picture-perfect. I snap a photo to send back to Brooklyn.

Crack!

Rustle.

Glancing left, I see the bear standing at the far end of the deck, where it meets the trail into the woods. Only 20 feet away, he stands motionless, staring at the sunset. I'm not sure he even notices me. I decide to slowly retreat inside and let him enjoy the moment. He doesn't have the luxury of watching from the kitchen. We stand gazing together, he outside on the deck, me by my kitchen table. When the sun fades, he turns and disappears into the forest.

I take a moment to reflect on the day and marvel at the spectacular beauty of this place we call home. I hope Squizz is curled up in his tree, nose tucked under his tail; I see the ruffled silhouette of Blue enjoying the sunset perched atop a cedar by the sea. I'm sure Red has already fluffed his feathers and settled into his comfy nest – he's the punctual type. Soon the bats emerge for twilight bug clean up. As their silhouettes zip and swoop at excessive speeds, I ponder how they avoid collisions without air traffic control.

Soon, the raccoons will be out, perhaps gazing at the stars or rolling up my neighbour's new turf. Everyone worked hard today. For now, I'm inside, grateful for the magic of a pink sky shared with all who call Howe Sound their home. Gazing at the pink highway to tomorrow, I exhale and smile.

WHERE THE MAGIC ONCE LIVED

Jenifer Dong

When I was five, my world was filled with the best things Barbies, dolls, and snacks. But nothing made me happier than daycare. It might sound weird to say I loved daycare, but it wasn't like regular school. It was way better. Daycare was fun and magical in a way that school could never be.

We got to wear princess dresses every day. Not just random ones, but the fancy, fluffy ones like in movies. There were tiaras and wands, too, and we'd twirl around pretending to be Cinderella or Belle. I felt like a real princess.

Snack time was another highlight. We had animal crackers, orange slices, and sometimes cookies. It was like a mini party every single day. We'd sit together, eating and laughing, and it was perfect.

Then there were water park days. Oh, my gosh, they were amazing! The teachers set up sprinklers and little slides, and we splashed around all afternoon. The smell of sunscreen and the chill of cold water on a hot day are memories I'll never forget. We laughed so hard my cheeks hurt. Daycare felt like the happiest place on earth.

But then I turned five, and everything changed. When you turn five, you go to kindergarten. Kindergarten isn't daycare. No princess dresses, no water park days, no free cookies. I thought it would be just as fun, but wow, was I wrong.

On the first day, I arrived with my sparkly princess backpack, ready for another magical day. But as soon as I walked in, I knew it wasn't the same. Nobody wore princess dresses. Everyone had on regular clothes – jeans and T-shirts. I felt so out of place.

Snack time was such a letdown. At daycare, snacks were awesome, but in kindergarten, you had to bring your own. My mom packed healthy stuff like carrot sticks and apple slices. It wasn't bad, but it wasn't *fun*. And nobody traded snacks or even talked much. Snack time felt so boring.

And don't get me started on nap time. At daycare, we lay on soft mats with blankets while lullabies played. It was my favourite part of the day. In kindergarten, nap time didn't exist. Instead, there was 'quiet time,' where you sat at your desk pretending to read. It was the worst.

Recess was okay, but it wasn't daycare-level fun. Sure, there were swings and a slide, but no water park. No sprinklers, no laughing until you couldn't breathe. Just kids running around. It felt like a downgrade.

Looking back, starting kindergarten wasn't just about going to a new school. It was about leaving behind the magic of being little. Kindergarten wasn't terrible, but it wasn't daycare, and that's what made it hard.

Even now, I think about those daycare days – the princess dresses, the snacks, the water park afternoons. It was all so perfect. I wish I could go back, even for one day, and relive it. Those were the best days ever.

FOF AND FOMO

John Weston

Some are motivated by FOMO (fear of missing out); I'm no exception. But I also battle FOF – fear of failure. Together, these fears propel me toward pursuing the long-term goals of both my personal journey and public mission.

The roots of my story reach back to World War II, when my father, Stan Weston, endured brutal conditions as a Japanese POW, suffering torture and every imaginable jungle disease. His captors withheld medication when he was sick. He was malnourished, and even had his appendix removed with a razor blade.

Growing up, I often wondered if I could have survived his 3 ½-year ordeal. His resilience shaped me. After the war, he rebuilt his life, developing a reputation as a top agricultural consultant to plantation owners on the Malay Peninsula. When he returned to British Columbia, he took on the challenge of transforming 1500 acres of undeveloped northern land into productive farmland. In 1958, the year I was born, he won the world championship for alfalfa. His expertise carried him around the globe, earning him the quirky accolade: "Stan can make grass grow on a golf ball."

If there's a trace of Dad's relentlessness in me, I guess that's not surprising, along with his need to tackle ambitious challenges – perhaps it's this same blend of FOF and FOMO that drives me toward distant horizons.

This instinct deepened in college when, in 1979, I joined BC's Department of Constitutional Affairs, where the province's representatives joined with Canadian leaders to draft our modern constitution. That summer job turned into a series of four summer jobs, where I absorbed the influence of constitution makers, people who, in their essence, thought long term.

From constitutional affairs, it was an obvious jump to law school. I practised in BC and Taiwan, taking time out to help open Canada's semi-diplomatic office in Taipei. Along the way, I started using my legal and diplomatic skills to help people wrongfully detained in foreign jails. This compulsion to help detained prisoners, I later realized, was my unconscious attempt to reach across time to help my father – even though I wasn't alive when he needed the help.

My drive found full expression when I represented Nisga'a elders in a decade-long legal battle over the role of

Canadian versus First Nations law. My clients asserted it was better for Canadian law to prevail, and the issue was key to the future of our country. I embarked on this epic legal challenge thinking it would take six months to get an expedited decision from the courts. Instead, we received two negative but diverse results from the lower courts, and the Supreme Court of Canada denied us leave to appeal. It's astonishing that, to this day, the critical issue remains unresolved. The battle is not over. The clients, who became close friends, are now working with me on a book about the struggle.

There was at least one significant positive consequence beyond the scope of the case itself. Determined to keep fighting for fundamental freedoms, I went to Washington, DC, where I spent three days shadowing leaders at the Institute for Justice. Using "IJ" as a model, I founded the Canadian Constitution Foundation (CCF), securing its charitable status and rallying for it resources for pro bono work. The CCF could litigate and educate, making it a pioneer on the Canadian landscape. Today, CCF stands as a leading defender of constitutional rights in Canada. As with any worthwhile endeavour, it's amazing how much time, effort, resources, and perseverance it takes to establish a sustainable non-profit enterprise.

FOF and FOMO converged again when I sought a seat in the House of Commons. Among other things, the role taught me to never let the lack of a title stop me from pursuing a worthy cause. Representing the region that hosted the 2010 Olympic and Paralympic Games – an experience that proved transformative – I saw the inspiring achievements of our athletes alongside troubling trends in national health.

Rising obesity rates, increasing youth depression, and sedentary lifestyles painted a grim picture. The statistics were alarming. Year after year, Canadians experience declining physical, mental, and spiritual health. Youth obesity is double what it was in 1979. Social media overexposure, loneliness, and outdoor impoverishment all play a role.

I wasn't the Minister of Health or the Minister of Sport – and no one specifically asked me to tackle the crisis in dwindling health capacity of average Canadians – but I couldn't just stand by and watch the problem fester. As MP, I worked with others to get bills passed – *Tackling Crystal Meth and Ecstasy* and *National Health and Fitness Day* – and initiated recurring events, such as Bike Day and Swim Day on the Hill. I got MPs of all parties to run and swim together, as role models for an increasingly sedentary nation.

These things had ceremonial significance but little effect in terms of measurable improvement in Canadians' health. More decisive action was necessary. So, after leaving parliament, I persuaded several passionate, influential Canadians to work with me to found the Canadian Health and Fitness Institute (CHFI). Our bold goal is to "Make Canada the Fittest Nation on Earth by 2030." Since 2017, our grueling journey has included financial hurdles and institutional resistance – I should have expected all that from founding the CCF, but some people are slow learners. Yet the stakes – reversing the

nation's decline in physical, mental, and spiritual health –
are too high for our team to abandon the effort.

One of my greatest inspirations was my friend Dr. Jack
Taunton, a pioneer in Canadian sport medicine and co-
founder of CHFI. Even while battling terminal illness,
Jack's resilience never wavered. A veteran of over 60
marathons, Jack had overcome polio as a kid. He started
the Vancouver Sun Run and the Vancouver Marathon and
served as Canada's top doctor in the 2010 Olympic Games.
Even when his strength was ebbing, he used poles to do
two-hour walks between medical procedures. He attended
almost every one of the 71 CHFI executive committee
meetings between 2017 and November 2024, when he
passed away.

Jack and I met a few weeks before he died. Frustrated
by the lack of support for our initiatives, I vented to him
over lunch. "We've donated thousands of hours of
volunteer time," I whined. "We have nine projects in hand
to promote measurable change. The country spent $344
billion last year on reactive healthcare, yet 1.6 million kids
are seeing therapists. Corporate sponsors are not showing
up. Donors are not arriving. Governments keep funding
their age-old, failing models." My whine became a full-
fledged lament. "Why is it so hard to make CHFI work?"

"The problem," Jack said, "is that you're not a
marathoner."

I'll never forget Jack's words. He was the living
embodiment of 'never give in' when pursuing a worthy
cause. His "you're not a marathoner" phrase was as close
to an admonishment as I'd ever received from him. In that

moment, I understood – it was time to recharge FOMO and FOF as engines of change.

FOMO – fear of missing out on a better future – and FOF – the fear of falling short – aren't just obstacles; they're fuel. If they've inspired me to keep going for the long haul, I'm sure they've inspired others, like Jack.

And so, I make this pledge: OK, Jack, I'm in it for the long haul. For all who've embarked on a worthy but difficult mission, may the FOMO and the FOF be with you!

A TRIBUTE TO MS. ROSS, THE TEACHER WHO CHANGED MY LIFE

Kate Huang

The first thing that comes to mind when I think of elementary school is changing schools in grade 6. Why? Because of my teacher. It might sound cheesy, but it's true. I will never forget my welcoming, hilarious, and inspiring grade 6 teacher, Ms. Ross.

From the moment I stepped into her classroom at West Bay Elementary, it felt like home. Ms. Ross had this way of making everyone feel comfortable, like they truly belonged. She was more than just a teacher – she was a shining light. She had a gift for making learning exciting, and her positive energy was infectious. She was like a rainbow on a rainy day, bringing hope and always finding the good in everything. She could brighten anyone's day with her smile and always made time for those who needed her.

Ms. Ross wasn't just a teacher; she was a mentor, a friend, and an inspiration. Her classroom was more than a place to learn; it was a safe space where we could be ourselves. She genuinely cared about her students, not just academically but personally. She knew how to make us laugh, challenge us, and comfort us when we were down. Her ability to connect with each of us was extraordinary. She even joked about being immortal because she was "too evil to die." We laughed at the time, not realizing how much we'd later wish it were true.

Sadly, on Halloween of 2024, Ms. Ross passed away. Her loss has left a deep void, but she will forever hold a special place in my heart. Every Halloween, I will remember her kindness, her laughter, and the joy she brought to so many. She will always be my favourite teacher, and my memories of her are among my most treasured.

In grade 6, I didn't enjoy playing outside during recess. Instead, I stayed in the classroom to help Ms. Ross. It wasn't about being a teacher's pet; I simply enjoyed spending time with her. She made everyone feel valued and supported, and her enthusiasm for life was contagious. Some of my favourite memories happened during snack and lunch breaks.

She would put on "The Daily Dose of Internet," and the whole class would laugh together. Sometimes, she'd hand out Jolly Ranchers or gummies and call them "healthy snacks" because, as she joked, "They came from the green Earth once!" Her humour made ordinary moments unforgettable.

During lunch, when the FIFA World Cup games were on, our class – along with students from another class – would gather to cheer for the teams. We even planned to attend the live event in 2026 when Canada hosts it.

Ms. Ross helped me build confidence and life skills I carry with me to this day, and for that, I will always be grateful. Math had always been a challenge for me, and I often doubted my abilities. But Ms. Ross taught me to persevere. She believed that anyone could succeed in math, and her encouragement motivated me to approach problems with determination. For the first time, I started to enjoy solving problems.

Ms. Ross had a way of making everyone feel special. Whether through her jokes, her encouragement, or simply her presence, she left a lasting mark on all of us. I feel so lucky to have spent a school year with her. The memories she created and the lessons she taught will stay with me forever.

Her impact went beyond the classroom. She taught me the importance of kindness, perseverance, and finding joy in the little things. She inspired me to be confident in myself and to approach life with an open heart and a positive attitude. She truly was one of the most thoughtful, kind, and inspiring people I have ever met.

Though she is no longer here, her legacy lives on in the hearts of her students. She will always be a beacon of hope and inspiration for me and many others. West Vancouver has been my home since 2019, and in that time, I have made many friends and had so many experiences. I am so grateful to live in such a welcoming and beautiful place. Thank you to West Vancouver and everyone in it for being a part of this journey.

Ms. Ross, you will always be remembered. Thank you for being the teacher who changed my life.

IT'S JUST A GAME

Kim Kiok Wong

It's a dark and stormy morning. A gaggle of early-bird seniors huddles outside the tennis center. At precisely 7 am the doors open, and we eagerly funnel in like cars merging onto the Lions Gate Bridge.

Some of us leave our extra baggage at the door.

We are dressed in various attire. On top of my salt-and-pepper hair, like a tiara, sits a cap embroidered with 'Queen of the Courts,' a prize for winning the Women's Singles Seniors Tennis Club championship. I wear a bright yellow T-shirt stamped with past 10K Sun Run accomplishments and a black mini skirt – the kind usually seen on young schoolgirls – which exposes my Snow White legs with topographic road maps etched on the backs of my thighs.

Unlike some of the others, I am missing the chic black accessories of tensor bands and braces around knees, elbows, and wrists, marks of a lifetime spent playing sport. As I only started playing sport in my forties, my body remains relatively intact.

Inside, the court resembles a cathedral, with the roof peaking at the center. Fluorescent lights bounce off the white ceiling. A large, frosted window on one side lets in muted light, and rain taps rhythmically on the metal roof. The court is glacier blue with white lines, surrounded by grass-green borders.

We hit balls back and forth gently to warm up stiff muscles and fragile joints. The balls trampoline off the strings like guitar plucks. Outside worries vanish; all our focus is within these walls.

"Have fun!" sets the tone as the game begins.

Serving seems simple: get the ball over the net into the serving box. But it is difficult to master. It is the only shot where you have total control – an empowering feeling. Noting my opponent's position, I decide where and how to serve. I adjust my grip, toss the ball high above my head, bring my racquet behind my back, swing it toward the falling ball, and propel my entire 100-pound body forward. This all happens within seconds. However, the fear of failure makes me tentative, and the ball hits the net.

In tennis, you get a second chance. This time, embracing the pressure and visualizing success, my serve is good and deep. I rush to the net. The opponents take advantage of my vertically challenged stature and lob it over my head. But Stan, my partner today, anticipates the lob. With years of experience, he moves slowly but with determination. "I think I can, I think I can," like Thomas the Tank Engine. He surprises everyone with an amazing shot, worthy of a 'highlights of tennis' segment on Sportsnet TV.

Stan yells, "Switch!"

Communication is key to success. Like Ginger Rogers and Fred Astaire, we crisscross the court gracefully, positioning ourselves for the next shot.

When the ball lands on their side, they call it out of bounds. It is close to the line but clearly in. We give them the benefit of the doubt and accept their call without protest. It's just a game.

Pressure is part of the game. When there is a tie and limited time, the next point wins. 'Sudden death' paralyzes some players. It is amazing how words affect the mind.

As Stan prepares to serve, he hesitates, unsure where to stand. He waits until everyone takes their position before choosing his spot. We wait patiently, perhaps seeing ourselves in him – a glimpse of the future.

"What's the score?" someone asks.

Blank faces meet the question.

We laugh, blaming 'senior moments' for our forgetfulness. Perhaps the real reason is we are not fully present. Our minds wander. *Did I lock the front door?* In the end, we agree to start over. Some players use gadgets on their racquets to keep score, relinquishing the need to use their brains, like smartphones. Ironically, these make us less smart.

When I focus, I am in the zone. The ball slows down, appearing as large as a beach ball. I can place it anywhere I want, feeling unbeatable. The score becomes crystal clear. When I lose focus, everything speeds up. The racquet and ball blur like lightning, the ball shrinks to the size of a ping pong ball, and I miss everything. I feel out of control, unable to remember the score.

The game continues. Our opponents hit the ball between us. "Down the middle solves the riddle," but we forget to communicate. We both go for the ball, and both miss. Stan, his own worst critic, berates himself.

"That's okay," I encourage. "You'll get it next time. One point at a time."

As a team, our goal is to set each other up for success.

At the end of the match, we gather at the net and tap racquets (a handshake before COVID-19, then tapping elbows or fists).

"Good game. That was fun."

Who won? It doesn't matter. We are winners for still being able to play this wonderful game.

We stay for coffee. I listen to players share stories of deceased spouses – their loneliness palpable. I share my joys and heartbreaks over my children and grandchildren. We exchange memories of parents and the values they passed down, now caring for them as roles reverse. I was blessed to have my mom until she was 100. Studies say racquet sports extend life by 9.5 years. Maybe I will play until I am 109. Age is relative – 55, 60, 70, 90 – it's just a number.

I am inspired by people's resilience: heart surgeries, cancer battles, one victory after another. We will have to be carried off the courts before we stop playing. We discover shared interests in gardening, music, hiking, and travel. Plans are made to meet outside of tennis.

As we leave, we glance at the frosted window that was dark earlier. The sun now casts a golden light, with silhouettes of trees creating a stained-glass effect. Some of us pick up the baggage we left at the door, all feeling lighter than when we arrived.

Tennis: is it just a game, or is it so much more?

DOWN

Laurisse Noël

It all makes its way down.

Rushes,
splashes,
drips,
slips,
pours,
soaks,
infuses and
leaks.
Seeps into crevasses
sneaking into the deepest of depths
Reaching to connect with more

More of its own.
More streams
Creeks
Rivers
Lakes
Seas
Oceans

The largest of rivers:
Fleuves (fr.)
It finds its way into those too
It finds more, then, when it is on its trundling way to places
most of us don't look
It is caught, as if plucked from its purpose of the down.
Roots grab on
They suck and slurp those drips and drops
They find the rain

The trickling veins of water are absorbed into their match
– the veins of roots pumping life into blooms
Thirsting for the hope of growth.

The washing of what is in the path is not lost.
The renewal that comes from gravity's pull on the wet.
It begs us to rethink our sandcastles,
our dirt piles,
our pollen
or anything that was carelessly tossed away, placed in the
path of a downpour.

There is much that may seem strong
Becoming permeable in nature
Vulnerable to the power of the pitter patter
Imbibing what it must
Satiated.

The rocks
Doing their best to stay
Forced out of their nests
But only at the fiercest of times
Reluctantly tumbling into new homes
Keen to be lodged with their fresh friends
For what could be an eternity…

Or at least until wandering eyes are drawn to them
"Ooh!" a fleeting instinct to grab it then squeeze
Cold seeping into fingertips
Warmth conducting into the core
Ground me
How long?
How long since you were in a volcano?
How long since you were squished into existence?
Bring me back to earth

The colours.
The rocks as a backdrop to what can be clear
A window into their symphony
Deep greens of the slow river
Meandering
Basking in pools

Heavy
Full
Reflecting the depth of the cosy forest
Shoulder to shoulder
Towering
Water
Disguised as its surroundings.

Splashes
Lapping
Thirst
Creatures
Quenched
Nothing beats that glacial runoff
Water is not meant to be in a shiny metal bowl
Sure steps on slippery rocks
Paw prints echo their passing
The river graced ever so briefly with their presence
They dart back into the trees
The smells
The sights and
Each other.

THE THINGS WE LEAVE UNSAID

Lindy Hughes Pfeil

Growing up, I often wished for a different kind of mother.

My father, on the other hand, was my hero. He shamelessly adored me and was proud of every little thing I did. I worshipped him.

In *West Vancouver Stories: The Pandemic Project* (the first volume of this series), I wrote about the little red record player Pa gave me for my thirteenth birthday and the music I listened to as a teenager: Joni James, Louis Armstrong, Frank Sinatra, Nat King Cole. My father's records, I said.

During the pandemic, as the world unravelled, it was my father's music that accompanied me on my daily walks through the neighbourhood. Pa had died thirty years earlier, but his hero status was undiminished. As I stomped along Marine Drive with Joni and Frank crooning through my AirPods, memories of my spectacular father danced along.

The Pandemic Project was published in February 2021. That June, my mother had a heart attack. I flew to South Africa with a copy in my hand luggage. Ma's recovery went smoothly – she is strong-willed, undramatic, and impatient. When I returned to West Vancouver a few weeks later, the book was on her bedside table. I never asked if she'd read my story. And she said nothing.

This was the hallmark of our relationship: saying nothing.

Ma came from hardy Afrikaner stock, where children were sometimes seen, never heard – unless limbs were broken, or blood stained the stinkwood floors. At fourteen, her father dropped dead of a heart attack, leaving her mother with four young children and a vineyard in the Western Cape. There was no time for drama.

Eight years later, my mother married my father, and when I arrived, she adopted the same no-nonsense approach to parenting. There was no warm and fuzzy with Ma. No cosy fireside chats where we shared our feelings. No "I love you." No gentle backrubs while tears flowed freely.

So many times, I wished Ma would say something. *Anything.* Like the day my ballet teacher broke it to me that I would never be good enough to be a ballerina. I shed my teenage tears quietly, in the dark of night, where no one would know. Ma remained silent. No words of comfort.

Or commiseration. When she packed away her tired sewing machine – the one that had turned sequins and tulle into tutus for me for more than a decade – I got the message. *Get over it.*

There were no conversations about life plans or hopes for the future. No words of wisdom.

With my ballerina dreams dashed, I opted for journalism. I'm not sure why. Four years later, my new degree in my back pocket, I applied to Boswell Wilkie Circus. Maybe I could be a juggler, an acrobat, a trapeze artist. It wasn't ballet, but there would be sparkly costumes and applause.

Ma didn't remind me that I had no eye-hand coordination or that I was terrified of heights. Nor did she point out that I had just spent a lot of my time and their money getting an education so that I *wouldn't* have to run away with the circus. She said nothing. Just let me get on with it.

The circus rejected me. Again, Ma said nothing.

I think she was happy when I found a 'real' job teaching English, though she didn't say so. After graduation, I'd moved back to my childhood bedroom overlooking the swimming pool and granadilla vines. This conveniently allowed me to spend my paycheck on tarot classes. (Perhaps my future lay in the cards.)

When I resigned from my real job a year later, to backpack across Europe, Ma didn't ask if this was a wise career move. Instead, she gifted me a deck of tarot cards and drove me to the airport.

While I was traveling, my father died, leaving my mother with no house and very little money. She packed her belongings in her little orange car and left Johannesburg, where she and Pa had built a life together – *our* life. She drove 1000 kilometres to a new city to forge a life of her own. No drama. She was just 50.

I fell into marriage, motherhood, and a house in the suburbs. When our children were toddlers, my husband and I decided to immigrate to Canada. Ma didn't try to change our minds. Didn't remind us of all the milestones she'd miss in her grandchildren's lives. She waved goodbye, didn't cry. Said nothing. Let us get on with it.

Being a mother turned out to be a lot trickier than I had anticipated. I told my children – all the time – that I was proud of them. That I loved them. Patted their backs. Let them cry. Still, motherhood was more confusing and heartbreaking than I ever imagined.

I discovered that saying nothing is sometimes very hard to do.

A few months after my last visit to South Africa – when I'd left behind *The Pandemic Project* – Ma died. Alone. No fuss. She just got on with it.

I flew back to pack up her life. That's when I discovered I'd gotten it all wrong. All those records – Joni James, Louis Armstrong, Frank Sinatra, Nat King Cole – had *Ma's* name written on the covers. Marlene Hugo. Before she met my father and became Marlene Hughes.

They were my *mother's* records. *Not* my father's.

And I pictured Ma leaving Johannesburg after Pa died, making space on the backseat of her little orange car –

between clothes and photo albums – for Joni, Frank, Louis, and Nat.

And I wondered: Did *Ma* give me the little red record player?

At her celebration of life, an old family friend I hadn't seen in decades said, "You always were a daddy's girl."

What did that mean? That I chose my father over my mother? That my mother knew?

I thought of the book on Ma's bedside table. I imagined her reading my story – the story about the records and the little red record player I had got all wrong – and saying … nothing.

It was her silence, I suddenly – *finally* – realized, that had given me the freedom to grab my dreams with both hands and run headlong into the universe – to figure out the world and my place in it. But it was also so much more. By saying nothing, my mother allowed my father to be my hero.

Perhaps love is not the words we speak out loud, but those we leave unsaid.

THE SIEVE

Lorraine Zander

"Toronto doesn't have this," Elizabeth says.

Her eyes sweep from Lions Gate Bridge to Vancouver Island, her face turned upward to capture the warmth of the fading sun. At 85, she stands tall and straight, gripping the weathered railing, facing south towards Spanish Banks Beach and the mountains beyond. We've paused along the Dundarave Seawall, where a copper fish weathervane marks a scenic viewing spot. I take a deep breath, inhaling mountain air mixed with a burst of ocean spray. A rejuvenating energy flows into my lungs and spreads through me.

Though I was born in Trinidad – a small Caribbean island known as the 'Land of the Hummingbird' –Toronto is where I made my forever friends, found my husband, and built a home. West Vancouver (apparently never to be mistakenly called Vancouver) was meant to be my temporary residence for six months. Elizabeth, recently widowed and living with mild dementia, needed support. My husband – her nephew – and I moved in to help.

Now, Elizabeth wants us to stay permanently.

Staring into the Burrard Inlet, I ignore the cargo ships and cruise liners, scanning the dark water for a bobbing seal, or better yet, the black dorsal fins of an orca pod. A few days ago, I saw a bald eagle land on a rocky outcrop near the pebbled shoreline. Larger than I expected, it carried itself with the grace of wildlife royalty. It was my first encounter with a wild eagle. As I focused on its white head and yellow beak (my husband's birding hobby has rubbed off on me), it swooped into the water, emerging with a fish skewered in its talons. Landing on another rock just feet from me, it began tearing into the fish while a hungry crow waited for scraps.

Elizabeth is right. Toronto doesn't have this.

Melodic notes from "When You Wish Upon a Star" blare from the horn of a Disney cruise ship heading to Alaska.

"I don't want to go on another cruise," Elizabeth says, pulling a soft silk scarf from around her neck, tucking it into her pocket.

"I thought you loved going on cruises," I say. "You told me the Alaskan cruise was one of your favourites."

"Really?" she says, still looking out at the ships. "I've been to Alaska?" She murmurs this more to herself than to me. Dementia has begun subtracting memories from her mind, reducing the sum of her rich, well-lived life.

Born in Germany in 1936 to parents who believed only boys needed a higher education, Elizabeth defied expectations, earning a master's degree in mathematics from Chicago's Northwestern University.

"Math was easy for me. The answers just popped into my mind," she'd say with a cheeky smile. "I graduated magna cum laude and beat all the boys."

We stand together a while longer. Then, as if energized by the sun, Elizabeth quickly turns from the railing, spreading her arms like a plane in flight. She begins heading back, laughing. I step in beside her.

My husband and I decide to stay, and for the next three years West Vancouver becomes our home.

Toronto's hustle and its sterile façade of skyscrapers and sidewalks are a blurry haze as the purples, reds, and oranges of the setting sun stretch across my patio. Elizabeth is cast in a soft glow.

"Tell me about Frank," I say, leaning down to adjust the blanket threatening to tangle in the spokes of her wheelchair. It's been over a year since her hip fracture left her unable to walk.

"Frank?" she echoes.

A gentle breeze brushes her hair across her face, but her late husband's name no longer lights up her features as it once did. Dementia continues pilfering her vast archive of experiences, robbing her of once-unforgettable moments. She doesn't recall being married in Siena, Italy, golfing in Palm Desert winters, or earning the nickname 'Wave

Runner' in a local paper that published a photo of her braving the seawall during a rainstorm.

We talk, laugh, and marvel at the hummingbirds dining at the feeder mere feet from us.

"Do you have room for chocolate chunk ice cream?" I ask.

It's a rhetorical question – it's her favourite dessert.

She unfolds a blue cloth napkin and places it neatly on her lap.

"I always have room for chocolate chunk ice cream," she says smiling.

Looking across the inlet, I reflect on cherished moments here: the eagle encounter, seeing orcas, hiking Cypress Mountain, and sitting outside The Music Box with my husband's arms around me as concert music wafted out.

I am privileged to live a life worth remembering. But as I glance at Elizabeth, I understand how fragile and precious memories are. Her life story is dimming a little more each day. Could this happen to me? I realize it already is. Some details of my stories are vague, moments are hazy, and experiences have vanished completely.

People reassure me that these lapses are 'normal,' yet part of me wants to hold onto every memory that has brought me joy or laughter. I want to lock them away, safe from the sieve of time. But I know that's not how it works. Fortunately, for every forgotten funny story, twice as many moments of pain and sadness fade too – and this brings me comfort.

Now, I focus on creating new experiences to replace the ones that will inevitably slip away. I know Elizabeth won't remember any of this tomorrow, but that's okay. Right now, we're laughing, savouring the creamy sweetness of ice cream, and basking in the sun's warm glow before it dips behind the mountains.

WINTER SOLSTICE IN THE SAND

Maja Rusinowska

It was December 21, the morning of the winter solstice. I sat at my desk, staring at my computer screen. The electronic document seemed as blank and uninspired as my thoughts. I sighed, tapping my fingers against the desk. My day job was competing with the thoughts and emotions stirring within me.

I picked up the black pen next to me, a comforting tool. I always keep a pen and notepad by my keyboard to capture my thoughts and ideas. Writing by hand – the act of jotting down notes and crossing things off a list – still holds meaning for me. The way the tiny ball of ink rolls across the pad feels purposeful.

But something deeper was vying for my attention, something I couldn't yet fully articulate. Subconsciously, I knew what it was, but consciously I was unsure. I took a deep breath, my stomach flipping, and exhaled slowly.

Through the sliding glass door, I gazed past my balcony – a personal oasis with plants and an L-shaped couch – and out to the water and horizon. The morning sky glowed with soft hues of pink, blue, and purple – a breathtaking west coast winter palette. A beautiful place to call home.

West Vancouver is not where I grew up; my childhood and early adulthood were spent in Toronto. But my heart always ached for a life on the West Coast. Watching the ships glide into Burrard Inlet, I savoured the moment. It beat looking out at the frosty 401 highway any day.

I moved here in 2019, and several things struck me right away.

First, the birds – they're enormous. The average West Coast seagull could swallow a scraggly Toronto gull whole. Maybe it's all the fresh salmon and shellfish. The birds are as robust and shiny as the Lululemon-clad pedestrians gracing the seawall.

Second, the streets and neighbourhoods grow remarkably dark after sunset.

"People sure do appreciate the shadows here," I'd say to anyone who would listen.

With fewer streetlights, the night sky reveals its wonders: the Pleiades, Orion, and Queen Cassiopeia greet you like old friends. Stargazing brings me joy.

Third, the drivers here are so relaxed. In Toronto, my hand always hovered over the horn. In West Vancouver, even the most obtuse driving behaviour is greeted with patience.

These memories made me smile until a flutter of anticipation stirred in my stomach again. That day, I was joining a new community – a circle of priestesses. Women celebrating the reclamation of feminine wisdom and power. Women who were knowledge seekers and healers. Together, we would honour the solstice, a special time to turn inward, slow down, and restore energy for renewal in the spring.

I was excited to meet these women, and to explore this growing part of myself that was ready to unravel. What a perfect time of year to begin – wrapped in warmth, lighting candles, eating nourishing soup, and embracing stillness. The sun, seemingly paused just above the horizon for three days, marked this moment of reflection. Darkness enveloped us, like being cradled in a vast cauldron.

The solstice ceremony was online. Women from around the world gathered to honour and express gratitude to the ancestors of the north, south, east and west. We sang, shared stories, and reflected deeply on the past year's journey. We set intentions for what to nurture during the solstice to cultivate and release in the spring. I left the ceremony grounded and grateful for the time spent with these women.

That evening, I ushered in the solstice with my mom and daughter on Dundarave Beach. We lit a fire in a portable fire pit, played soft music, and roasted marshmallows under cosy hats and blankets. Above us, the Pleiades, Orion, and Queen Cassiopeia sparkled, while the tanker lights twinkled in the distance. As I dug my bare toes into the sand, connecting with the earth, gratitude overwhelmed me. It was a moment I won't soon forget. The firelight danced across our smiling faces, three generations of women together. In that moment, I thought, we are all priestesses.

UNFOLDING OF LIFE'S MYSTERIES ON AMBLESIDE BEACH

Marianne Pengelly

I first encountered the ocean in 1969. A girl from the prairies and a representative for the University of Calgary student newspaper, I was attending a conference at the University of British Columbia. Late in the evening, I finally stood on the shore, listening to the gentle splash of waves. The grey hood of the sky loomed over the ocean like a clamshell. I was on the edge of something immense, alive, and mysterious. The draw of the sea inspired my move to Vancouver in 1972.

During COVID-19, I committed to 50 days of beach cleaning to raise funds for vulnerable African children. My experiences at the beach were so fascinating, I have continued. Ambleside Beach, my backyard, became my sanctuary. The curve of the beach is anchored at one end by the open arms of the Squamish Nation Welcome Figure at the harbour entrance, and at the other end by the weathered poles of the Fourteenth Street pier. Burrard Inlet's waters lap against the soft brown sand.

When I breathe the salt air, I relax and let my burdens fall. Like life, the beach is an ever-changing canvas, offering beauty and brokenness. Like the ocean, I churn things over, reflecting on movement and impermanence.

What will I find today? What lies hidden among the logs piled high during winter storms? I patrol the beach with my blue 'I Love Oceans' collection bag and long-handled tongs. I remove debris that will harm sea life: bottle caps, bits of plastic, rusted cigarette lighters, toothbrushes, masks, balls, plastic ties, rope, and slabs of mussel-encrusted Styrofoam.

Over the years, I've discovered a copper-bottomed cooking pot without a handle, a cell phone, eyeglasses without lenses, and a 10-inch plaster chess piece. Objects slip through our fingers with careless ease. They lie tangled among two categories of natural beach debris. First is the bull kelp, bladderwrack, seagrass, rough patches of Turkish washcloth, or the black tangles of witch's hair. Then there are piles of sticks, bark, leaves, and millions of gull feathers discarded during the fall moulting season. Some finds surprise me – shotgun casings. Others shock me – syringes. Some sadden me, like secret messages left behind.

Often there are flowers. Today, I retrieved a yellow rose preserved in dry sand. Once, I found a message stapled to a log: "Luna, we love and miss you," alongside a bouquet of daisies that lingered for weeks before the ocean claimed them. Who was Luna? Petals of roses, daisies, and hydrangeas scattered on the shore are symbols of grief, love, and memory. The beach mirrors life, as the ocean delivers joy and sorrow and sweeps it away.

Loss marks childhood, and the beach collects children's forgotten belongings: jackets, caps, socks, shoes, buckets, shovels, trucks, action figures, a rubber Gila monster, a blue pony, pencils, markers, and painted rocks. I've decorated rocks myself, like the one on which I painted 'HOPE' and added to a display of two dolls dressed in red. Someone had wedged them into the roots of a silvered driftwood stump – symbols of pain, of missing and murdered Indigenous women and girls. The dolls stayed for weeks. HOPE disappeared within days.

While fundraising through beach cleaning, I created art tableaus with found pieces, photographed and posted them online. The beach reveals figurative and literal fragments of life. Once, a woman's anger lingered in the air after she wrote her story on a plate and smashed it against boulders. I collected the shards into a poem:

Among granite boulders
lie jagged shards –
sorrow in black marker

on a white plate: 'Casa Moderna'
caught between the cracks.
Someone's suffering
and messages:
"I still don't," "Better to cope…"
"Forever doesn't…"
Dreams –

        served

            hurled

                shattered.

Loss of a relationship was one fragment. Another time, it was loss of a person. Of all the stories I've encountered, Chelsea Poorman's has affected me the most.

I met Chelsea's sister, Amber, on the beach. She donated to my beach-cleaning project and shared her story. Amber and her father, Mike, from Saskatoon, had spent seven months searching for Chelsea, who had vanished one evening from Granville Street. The last Amber had heard from her sister was a cut-off phone call. Their sorrow touched me. I, too, have a dear sister and cannot imagine losing her. I offered to distribute missing-person posters and kept in touch via social media, witnessing their love in action.

Six months passed. They posted an invitation to a rally.

It is one thing to hear news reports about missing and murdered Indigenous women and girls and another to step into their world in solidarity. Marchers wearing ribbon skirts, cedar hats, and red T-shirts bearing Chelsea's image walked down Granville Street. A long red banner read

'Bring Chelsea Home.' At Georgia and Granville, they formed a circle. A matriarch with silver hair introduced Chelsea's mother to each person. The matriarch radiated energy, but I felt Mrs. Poorman's exhaustion as I held her hand. Participants stepped into the circle to speak, sing, drum, or share messages of grief, support, and anger.

A year after I met Mike and Amber, Chelsea's remains were discovered in an empty Shaughnessy mansion. The police initially declared her death 'not suspicious,' leaving bitterness in its wake. The family's story ebbs and flows, as they continue seeking justice, a tide far from shore.

One low-tide day, I spotted a turquoise rock far out in the channel. On it was written: "I lay this rock for you. This is the spot where my memory of you hits my heart." I returned the rock, its tender secret intact.

Another time, I found a message I thought was meant for me. I stumbled upon a pale blue plastic container the size of a deck of cards. It turned out to be a toy with white hands and feet, and the letters L. I. F. E printed above its face. It made me laugh. That is my experience of beach cleaning – life *is* at my feet.

Like life, the beach holds secrets, reveals them, and reclaims them. It connects me to the natural, material, and spiritual worlds. The ocean washes the beach twice daily, erasing footprints and past deposits while welcoming the next. It cleanses me. Old stories vanish, and new ones sweep in, deepening my beach-life connection.

MAEVE

Monica Higgins

The eagles are calling me. I grab my binoculars and head to the secret beach. What will I learn today? Where is the best vantage point to observe them? Should I brave the steep, rickety stairs or lurk at the top of the nest-tree driveway? My curiosity pulls me to the green fence.

The best view of the nest is behind the tall green door that leads to another era – the hippy days of my youth. I yank open the heavy wooden portal, hoping no one hears the dull thud as it slams behind me. Instead of a forest floor or rocky outcrops, I'm on a cracked slab of pavement. Moss, ferns, and ivy thrive in the cracks – fluffy volcanoes of life.

To my left, an old car rests, its windows and roof coated in algae. The tires sag, as though content in this tranquil spot far from highways and horns. Between the arbutus branches, the Salish Sea, Passage Island, and Vancouver Island shimmer in the distance.

Just beyond the branches, about five metres away, sits the only eagle nest on the North Shore that is visible at eye level. Built in an old Douglas fir, the massive nest of sticks and branches houses the eagles I monitor. Nearby, a solitary pole still stands, its rusted hook a remnant of a tetherball game.

From this forgotten playground, I have a clear view of the nest. When the eaglets grow tall enough, binoculars aren't necessary. How close can I get without disturbing them? Sally, the director of the North Shore Eagle Network, sets the boundaries: I don't cross the ivy line. Monitoring the eagles means collecting data and reporting to Sally about the phases of their lives. When the eagles communicate, I hear them – wherever they are – and that means I'm on call.

When the eagle pair begin renovating the nest, it signals family planning. I record egg-laying dates, hatching times, number of young, and feeding habits. The seasons of eagle life are predictable, but suspense is constant.

Drama unfolds when eaglets test their wings, wobbling on the nest's edge. It's nail-biting to watch. Some eaglets fall, surviving days on the ground before making their way home. If an eaglet goes missing, I alert Sally, who contacts OWL, a non-profit that rescues injured or orphaned raptors.

The parent eagles, Eagle Eye (or Jimmy) and Harbour Sun, love their waterfront nest. They trade off sitting on eggs, their gazes fixed on the ocean. The ever-changing tides, colours, and textures provide a backdrop of endless activity: picnickers, dogs, kayakers, Sea-Doos, boats, and crows seeking revenge for lost eggs or chicks.

After the eggs hatch, survival is never guaranteed. One day, I spied Jimmy Junior, the 2023 eaglet, pecking at his younger, smaller sibling. It was tempting to hurl a pinecone at him, but I paused, acknowledging nature's harsh rule of survival of the fittest: why share food when you can have it all?

The day we realized there was only one eaglet in the nest was heartbreaking. We were powerless, as a search under the nest was not possible on the steep, rocky cliff.

When eagle drama occurs, I text Sally right away, always impressed by her quick attention to all eagle matters. The cunning Jimmy Junior, sole-surviving eaglet that year, grew from an ET-looking creature into a mottled brown, black, and white eaglet. He stretched his wings while waiting for food to be delivered straight to his beak. Mom and Dad fed him this way right up to his departure. In preparation for his first flight, Jimmy Junior would tentatively step onto a branch and work his way up to hopping about on the branches that held up his home.

The eagles always know I'm there, acknowledging me with a piercing stare.

During the 2024 season, a fellow monitor suggested naming the new eaglet Maeve. After a string of males, it was time for a girl.

Maeve's personality was revealed when it was time for her to practice flying. While other eaglets took flight, Maeve lounged in her nest, watching the clouds. She wasn't in a rush to leave the comfort of her childhood nest. She did not seem to care that all the other North Shore eagles had fledged and were on their journey north. Finally, at the last moment, she took a short flight to a nearby tree. A few days later, Maeve was gone.

It's bittersweet when the eaglets leave, but they'll return to this coastal paradise in a few months.

Monitoring eagles is a natural way to immerse myself in nature. Since 2019, our team has grown from just me to seven community members observing from different vantage points in the neighbourhood. While the eagles scan the Salish Sea for food and danger, we scan for signs of their lives.

Protecting these magnificent birds has become my passion. When I see them soaring, part of me is up there with them, on the wings of the wind.

AMBLESIDE IS CONTEMPORARY ITHAKA

Patricia L. Morris

As you set out for Ambleside
hope your road is a long one,
full of adventure, full of discovery.
Doubts — don't fear them;
they'll fade if your thoughts are elsewhere.
Always, keep Ambleside in your mind
arriving is something you're destined for

And hope your road is a long one.
May there be many summer mornings when
with joy and wonder, you enter new harbours

to stroll the twenty kilometres of shoreline.
May you crab the pier, manicure on Marine Dr.
and may you walk to the library
to glean algorithms from knowledge-keepers.

Always, keep Ambleside in your mind.
Arriving there is what you're fated for.
But don't hurry the journey at all.
Better if it lasts for years.

Ambleside gives you everything,
nothing left to give you now.
Wise as you'll become, rich with experience,
you understand – Ambleside is Ithaka reimagined.

(Borrowed and adapted with permission from C. P. Cavafy)

From ridiculous to sublime

Three years ago, I moved ten kilometers to the village of West Vancouver, leaving behind two decades in the Downtown Eastside. From Canada's poorest postal code to one of its wealthiest. I sold my four-story treehouse on Alexander Street for a seniors' co-op apartment on 14th in Ambleside. The vinyl-sided exterior whispers "ordinary," but inside, there's promise.

Location, location, location. Moving smaller to feel bigger, moving older to be renewed.

We are never *of* one place. I've called Winnipeg, Roseisle (Manitoba), Toronto, Cambridge (Massachusetts), Halifax, and Madang (Papua New Guinea) home. Home is not a destination; it's all the journeys between and the reflections they inspire.

Life at Ambleside

I stand on one leg, a heron on the water's edge, the silent reflection my only companion. Paddleboarders glide through the Pacific light as winds etch patterns on the ocean's surface. On my paddleboard, I find freedom – illegal between the bridges.

I cycle to hike, microspiking high in old snow on Cypress Mountain, no longer content to admire the magnificent Lions from afar. My grey hair earns nods of respect, not suspicion. Here I am not "other," not a gentrifier. I puddle-jump through muddy rain to aquafit class, passing a man feeding crows at a rushing creek – a small act of grace.

It's a twenty-minute seawall stroll to the West Vancouver Memorial library, where bookish wooden figures, Mr. and Mrs. Carver Plumtree, greet me. My former library route meant navigating feces, shopping carts, and human despair on Hastings Street.

Empowered explorations

Fifty years ago, my instructor with a full darkroom baked Scotch eggs for me on Inglewood Avenue. Back then my wild heart scoffed at suburbia. Now, Ambleside empowers me. It entitles me, too. The privilege of living in this bubble feels both earned and uneasy. Shadows of uncertainty linger. It is part of the deal.

On Saturday mornings, I kayak with Women on Water, paddling west. An ophthalmologist in the group gifted me new lenses for my cataracts – full-spectrum clarity to see the world anew.

My neighbour Bruce – a former student from the elementary school where I watch 'kiss and drive' parents drop their kids – pointed me to the *I Grew Up in West Vancouver* Facebook page. They ask: "Where else would you possibly want to be?"

The Hollyburn Sailing Club, at the foot of my street, is my happy place. They named me 2024 Paddler of the Year. I celebrated my birthday there this October. Rain pelted as crepes were served from the food truck, sailors raced, then a double rainbow arched over the east. As the band played "Rollin' Cross A River," a sliver of moon hung over Stanley Park. This is, indeed, my last resort.

Ambleside's whispers

On the inflatable *Lingcod*, I paddle under the pier, where algae-barnacled pilings form lacework. Crabs tap their dreams, and ghosts of the sea whisper through clicking claws.

The poet with stones has moved her monoliths. The sea will destroy them. I saw the clan in all its beauty – birds, animals, and abstracts piled high. Enhancing the humans. Or are they human? What is human? That young woman jogging for her life? The older woman talking with her Yorkie?

Further west, I navigate kelp beds and the shiny shoreline, gliding past vacant glass mansions. Seals lounge, tough-skinned and grey as the bay. Freighters cut silently through soup-coloured water as wind slaps my face awake.

I follow my personal dark cloud until it passes in a high wind. Paddleboarding is incomparable intercourse. It balances me. From the sea, I see the bridge strung with lights, a gift to West Vancouver's night sky. Strung tighter than a piano, she's tuned to both shores – nightmarish, the idea you can't get across, slight, and anachronistic.

Friends claim it's longer to drive to West Vancouver than it is for me to visit them. I take the #257 bus, travelling from clipped poodles to graffiti-marked black lab territory. The Squamish Nation Welcome Figure drums me back. It's more than a landing – it's the wanderings.

The Spirit Bike Trail runs beside the Squamish reserve, leading me to a summer powwow where dancers move to rhythms that transcend time. I bike by Sandy Cove, where Indigenous history meets settler tales. At Lighthouse Park, ancient Douglas firs stand sentinel over this ever-changing coast. Movement is healing. After my 2023 bicycle accident, I test my balance and strength among the rocks, grateful to be spared. At least for now.

Reflections on change

I read to understand the climate changes engulfing us. My goal is to live long enough to ask, "Where were you when?" Last month, 292 mm of rain fell in an atmospheric river, turning roads into rivers. Spring brings fires that burn too long.

Mrs. Plumtree, carved in 1977, clutches her *Cast Iron Cooking* book while children play beneath her refurnished skirt. Like her, I adapt. Recreated by time, puzzled by the future, I dream of robots to help me age into decrepitude.

I grow comfortable with people I might never have met if not for shared geography.

I put on weight in some places, lose too much in others. Though my injuries have largely healed, I am still cracked and vulnerable, like a cup with a glued-on handle. Some say there's beauty in cracks – cracks are how the light gets in. But more significantly, it's how Cavafy's poem infuses life into my journeys as it seeps in – reclaiming Ambleside as Ithaka, a place not of arrival but of countless journeys.

JOURNEY THROUGH TIME WITH MISTY
(April 12, 2010 – April 12, 2024)

Shideh Khorasheh

Misty came into my life while I was living in Stamford, Connecticut. A few months earlier, I had noticed my neighbour Elena's fluffy white dog, Brittany, a toy Maltese. Brittany brought Elena so much joy that I decided I wanted a toy Maltese too.

On Sunday, June 13, 2010, Elena and I drove the hour and a half to Brooklyn, New York, where she had purchased Brittany.

"How will I know which dog to choose?" I kept asking. Elena laughed. "Don't worry, the dog will choose you."

This would be my first dog, and I already had a name in mind – Misty. I wanted a name that started with the same letter as my mom's name, Mahin, whom I had lost eight years earlier.

At Puppy's Boutique, five puppies were brought out. Only one showed any interest in me. She sat by my leg and began to shake. When the puppies were returned to their crate, she stuck her nose out and stared at me.

"This is a no brainer," said Elena. "The dog has chosen you."

Misty.

I brought her home, unaware that this three-pound fluffy, white angel, small enough to fit in the palm of my hand, would change my life forever.

The next day, I had to work and couldn't leave Misty home alone. I put her in the bag I had purchased for her and took her to the office. When my boss, Catherine, arrived, I asked her to come to my office. I unzipped the bag, and Misty emerged – then promptly peed on the carpet.

From then on, Misty went everywhere with me – the gym, the mall, work, movies, church. In October 2013, when Misty was three, we took an unforgettable road trip to Vermont to see the foliage. Her sweet soul and big personality brought smiles to everyone she met.

In December 2015, I moved back to West Vancouver to be with my dad and my brother who has special needs. Misty and I moved into my dad's home, where he lovingly referred to her as "the blessing of the house." When my dad passed away in August 2018, both Misty and I mourned deeply.

In spring of 2019, I discovered the St. John Ambulance Therapy Dog program. Misty fit all the requirements, and after evaluation, she began touching lives across the North Shore. For five years, she brought comfort to adults with special needs, residents of nursing homes, students, and people in hospice care. The world, specially mine, was brighter because of Misty. My dad always said she had a way of knowing who needed her most.

Two of Misty's favourite places were West Vancouver Memorial Library and Capilano University. At the library, she would wag her tail as we entered, heading straight to the second-floor room where children read to her. She brought joy to so many kids, and through her therapy dog adventures, I met incredible people.

In July 2019, when Misty was nine, we embarked on a 12-day road trip with Jane Adams Clark, a North Shore artist who was 90 at the time. Jane wanted to paint glaciers, and Misty became our trip mascot. During the journey, we even attended Bryan Adams' outdoor concert in Fort MacMurray, Alberta,

Misty stood by me through life's hardest moments, bringing healing and comfort. She helped me cope with the loss of my dad, several dear friends, and Mrs. Nickel, who passed away in December 2022.

Mrs. Nickel had been in my life for 43 years, ever since I moved from Iran to Winnipeg in 1979 and attended Balmoral Hall boarding school. She was my art teacher and a second mother to me during the years I couldn't see my own mom due to the Iran-Iraq war. When Mrs. Nickel died on December 8, 2022, just 10 hours after I arrived in Winnipeg to visit her, I was devastated. Misty played a vital role in my healing.

Everything changed on September 29, 2023. We were volunteering at the West Vancouver Memorial Library that afternoon. That evening, Misty had her first episode of heart failure. I took her to the emergency vet and managed to keep her alive for another six and a half months, standing by her as she had always stood by me. But on April 12, 2024 – her fourteenth birthday – I had to say goodbye.

It was one of the hardest days of my life. Anyone who has had to say goodbye to a beloved pet will understand. Misty was more than a dog; she was my soulmate, companion, best friend, and the child I had never had.

My life has been forever changed by Misty's unconditional love, joy, and healing presence. The best thing that ever happened to me, my precious Misty will live in my heart forever.

A SEAWALL OF MEMORIES

Victoria Klassen

Waves lapped against the shore as I walked along the path with my great-uncle. His puffer jacket was zipped up all the way despite the beautiful September day. I was enjoying the unseasonably warm weather for September – or so I'd been told. I'd only moved to Vancouver a week earlier to begin a master's program.

"We used to start at 24th and walk all the way down the seawall and back. But we won't go that far today," my uncle said. We were starting our walk at the opposite end of his usual route.

After my arrival in Vancouver, I'd been spending time with him. On this day, after running errands together and grabbing lunch at Park Royal, he suggested a walk along the seawall.

We veered off the path and down the fishing pier, where a fisherman was pulling up a net. A large crab wriggled free, landing with a plunk on the soggy dock. Nearby, a little girl pointed and shrieked.

"They have to be a certain size," my uncle explained, as the fisherman took out a tool to measure the crab. We walked to the shore, past the community gardens and flower beds, and back onto the path.

A month later, with my little sister Sarah by my side, we walked at a brisker pace along the seawall. She was visiting during her fall reading week. After three days of unrelenting rain – and a leaky roof – we finally managed to get out for a walk during a break in weather.

I led us to the Grassquatch, an enormous art installation that had made me smile the first time I saw it. The seated sasquatch, covered in scraggly grass, had oversized feet sticking out.

"Wouldn't Nancy love this?" I asked Sarah. Nancy was Sarah's mom and my stepmom.

"Oh yeah," Sarah agreed. She crouched down, posing in front of the Grassquatch, and I snapped a few photos to send to Nancy and our dad.

The sumac bushes along the path were turning a vibrant red. We walked through the community gardens, admiring the flowers still in bloom even though it was mid-October.

We arrived at a plot that must have once grown garlic. A handwritten sign read: *Whoever stole all my garlic is a creep.*

We laughed, wondering who needed that much garlic.

The next time I went down to the seawall, alone, crashing waves greeted me. After Sarah's visit, the first twinges of homesickness had begun to stir in my belly. The sun peeked out behind grey skies, and I lifted my face to soak in the rays. Between the sunshine and the waves, this walk lifted my spirits. It reminded me how lucky I was to spend a year in this beautiful place – close to the ocean, mountains, and sparkling city lights.

It was easy to picture my great-uncle walking hand in hand with his wife along this same seawall.

"This is what my wife is missing," my uncle had said during our September stroll. "These walks. We walked along here every day after dinner."

"How long did it take you?" I asked as we passed the creek with signs about salmon.

"Oh, we didn't rush. An hour or two, and we watched the sun set."

Our walk together along the seawall that day, I realized, had been a walk down memory lane for him. His wife's illness had ended their days of walking the seawall together.

Today, as I walk hand in hand along the seawall with my partner, Rob, I can't help but think of my uncle and his wife. Rob is visiting from our home in Ottawa for the week. I was excited to bring him to the seawall partly because I knew my uncle wanted Rob and me to share in the joy these walks brought him and his wife for so many years.

As much as I have been enjoying Vancouver – settling into my classes, making new friends, and exploring the city – with Rob by my side, my piece of home is with me.

We walk out onto a dock, pausing to take in the glittering surface of the ocean, dotted with boats. As the sun begins to dip, the golden hour glow lights up Rob's face. I soak in the moment. What a gift it is to be present with those you love.

With salt on the breeze, waves crashing against the shore, and our fingers intertwined, we continue to walk along the seawall, making memories with each step.

THE JOY OF BEING FEARLESS

Wendy Wilkins Winslow

Joy has come to me in different ways, shapes, and sizes at different times in my life. One of my current joys is five foot ten. She comes dressed in sequinned bodysuits, sparkly blazers, princess dresses, and flowing capes. She wears custom Louboutin thigh-high boots and sings in a mezzo-soprano voice that's easy to sing along with. Tens of thousands of people, mostly teenaged girls, know all the lyrics to all her songs and belt them out as though they, too, are on the stage. It always seems as though the audience, as well as the singers and dancers on stage, are having a fabulous time.

She writes her own music and lyrics. And her most recent Eras Tour spanned 149 concerts across five continents. Each show, a high-energy, three-hour spectacle, brings immense joy to the 70,000 fans in the audience. Her songs resonate with teenage girls capturing their lives, their loves, their heartbreaks. Her accolades include 58 Grammy nominations, 14 wins, and a record four Album of the Year awards.

Her every move, especially her romantic relationships, is scrutinised by fans and the media. She's a billionaire, earning over $18 million CAD per concert, according to *Forbes*.

She is of course, Taylor Swift. Global pop star and cultural phenomenon is what we see. But there is a lot we don't see. Taylor Swift is much more than meets the eye.

Beyond the glitz and glamour lies her philanthropy, much of it done without fanfare or seeking recognition. She uses her wealth to bring joy to individuals, foundations, communities, and cities. At the individual level, she gave $100,000 bonuses to each of the 50 truck drivers who transported her set during the tour – a gesture some described as "life-changing." She has also given generous bonuses to her dancers, musicians, caterers, and technicians. Taylor has provided financial support to families grappling with overwhelming medical bills, autism, cancer, and other personal crises.

At the organizational level, her contributions span disaster relief, food banks, educational programs, cancer research, and sexual assault advocacy. Her economic impact on cities during the tour is staggering – an estimated $158 million in Vancouver alone.

Taylor's influence extends beyond philanthropy. Prestigious universities like Harvard, Stanford and Queen's offer Swift-related courses in subjects as varied as English, political science, and business. She is also a strong role model for teenage girls, using her platform to empower them. In 2022, NYU awarded her an honorary Doctor of Fine Arts. Her commencement address reflected on life lessons about love, criticism, choices, public humiliation, hope, and friendship.

At the 2016 Grammys, she encouraged young women: "There are going to be people along the way who will try to undercut your success or take credit for your accomplishments or your fame, but if you just focus on the work and you don't let those people sidetrack you, someday when you get where you're going you'll look around and you will know that it was you and the people who love you who put you there. And that will be the greatest feeling in the world."

In December 2024, Vancouver celebrated the three final Eras Tour concerts. The West Vancouver Memorial Library organized a *Swifties Fan Meetup*. In North Vancouver, the Capilano Suspension Bridge was turned into a giant friendship bracelet with the word FEARLESS swaying from the bridge, not a crossing for the fearful. Gastown's iconic steam clock chimed "Shake it Off" every fifteen minutes and Vancouver police horses deployed around the concert venue wore giant friendship bracelets around their necks.

My California granddaughters are two of those ensorcelled teenagers. Taylor would like them. They are beautiful people and the best of friends. Both are tall, kind, and smart. They volunteer, do well at school, and have plans for university. They FaceTime regularly with their grandmother. They both have long dark hair and big brown eyes with eyelashes that I covet.

Recently they attended a Taylor Swift concert in Los Angeles with their mother and two friends. Mum, unwilling to pay scalper prices, had spent many, many hours on hold to buy the tickets. The girls spent weeks planning their Swift-inspired outfits – micro skirts, glamorous tops, and knee-high sparkly boots. They made dozens of friendships bracelets to share with other Swifties at the concert. Excitement was high!

As the concert started, they sent me a video of them singing, laughing, shrieking with unapologetic joy. They were having a blast and everyone around felt the same. Endorphins were flowing.

But apparently you can only shriek for so long. Midway through the third hour, my 16-year-old granddaughter developed a violent case of hiccups. They were so loud and unrelenting that she had to lie down with her head on her mother's knee. It would have been terribly embarrassing if she hadn't felt so sick. After the concert she threw up in the parking lot and then announced: "It was the best day ever!"

Joy, it seems, can transcend external circumstances.

THE HIMALAYAS

Yasmin Vejs Simsek

It's a brisk morning, unusual for the typically humid Nepalese weather. For once, it's comfortable being outside, but it has yet to hit 8 am and the heat will surely reach the mountains in the next few hours. The only sounds are the wind in the trees, the sweet music of the wind chimes from the little market down the dirt road, and the occasional contented moo of cows grazing nearby.

I sit barefoot and cross-legged, the grass slightly damp beneath my shorts, close to my favourite cow (who I've aptly named Milky). Milky and I have developed a comfortable bond over the past three weeks – ever since I started meditating here each morning. I feed her some hay, and she swats mosquitos away from me with her tail – what I can only assume is a declaration of love in cow world.

Her fellow cows graze nearby, embodying the mindfulness I am seeking. The Himalayas form a beautiful backdrop of serenity to engage in empty thoughts. The mountains are painted on the clearest of blue skies and surrounded by trees larger and more vibrantly green than I've ever seen. But none of it feels overwhelming. It feels calm. It feels like mine.

As I settle into meditation, I focus on letting go of my thoughts. This hasn't been easy – I tend to dwell in my head more than my heart. Over the past few weeks, life in the mountains has helped me embrace a slower pace, but today my mind is restless, scrambled by the phone call I received in the quiet of the night.

Falling asleep had been difficult enough. After the call, I considered every possible line of action. Should I go home? I've barely been here a month – how can I leave so soon, abandoning a four-month project? But how can I stay, leaving my father to fend for himself? The values I was raised with, the values I've been rediscovering here, leave no room for turning my back on family.

The people in Bhotang live by a deep sense of community, kindness, and shared responsibility – principles I came here to reconnect with, and morals I want to live by.

Reconnecting with Narayen 10 years after we first met at university has allowed me to sink into the sense of safety I felt with him all those years ago. His family and coworkers have taught me to clear my mind and embrace the meditation practice Milky and I share every morning. They've also reminded me of the problems of my Western mindset – the illusion of independence and self-reliance.

Here, people understand that every struggle is shared, and harmony comes from facing challenges together. Someone will always catch you if you fall; someone will always hold your deepest thoughts as their own. That is peace.

I realise the only way forward is to embody these lessons and support my father. But for now, I owe it to myself – and Milky – to stay present in this moment. Release all thoughts. Be in the now. *Viśrāma.*

After half an hour, I stand, light-headed and dizzy. I hold on to Milky to regain my balance and she stares at me with her unbothered gaze and kind eyes. Then I walk down the hill with the kind of clarity that comes from releasing past traumas and letting go of future worries, even just for a moment.

In my room, I pack quickly, determined to catch the hourly bus to town and buy a plane ticket. From there, I'll head to Kathmandu and fly home. I should arrive somctime tomorrow. Bag in hand, I walk to the office, where Narayen is working.

I knock. Narayen welcomes me in with a smile, and I tell him about the phone call.

"I'm sorry I won't be able to finish the research here," I say. "Thank you for welcoming me into your family and community, I really appreciate your generosity. I've loved reconnecting with you, and I hope to return one day to continue working on this project – and myself."

"Nadia, there's no need to apologise," he says. "Family comes first. You must be with the people you love in times of need, or you'll end up leading a lonely life. You and I are part of each other's community, no matter where we are. Once you're woven into someone's fabric, you'll forever be part of their life pattern. You're always welcome here."

He hugs me, bringing tears to my eyes. I shut them to avoid becoming more emotional than I already am. I like Narayen – how calm I feel around him. I admire the peace and confidence he exudes – it's something I need now more than ever.

As I leave, I glance back at the building, feeling a bittersweet sense of sadness and contentment.

I will be back.

Author Note: This story is semi-autobiographical, and names and details have been altered.

ABOUT THE WRITERS

ANNE BAIRD is the author of 11 illustrated children's books (William Morrow and Simon and Schuster.) She created *Goddess Cards, eGoddess Cards*, and *Little Big Books*. She writes and illustrates for the *Beacon* newspaper and has been writing and illustrating since childhood. amazon.com/stores/AnneBaird/author/B001HOWK3S

ANNE LABELLE has lived in the postcard community of West Vancouver since 2000. A geologist, lawyer, and corporate director, she has worked throughout Canada, including all three Arctic territories. Anne enjoys activities outdoors (skiing, canoeing, camping, and gardening) and indoors (pottery, woodworking, knitting, and sewing), but most of all enjoys spending time with her extended, blended family. She is the willing servant of two black cats, brothers Raven and Smoochie, adopted from the West Vancouver branch of the BC SPCA, where she is a dedicated volunteer.

BRENDA MORRISON grew up wandering the hills and shores of West Vancouver. Her heart sang a deep song when her adventurous spirit brought her home to raise her children, Hamish and Anna, close to the land and the family she holds dear. Her life's work is centred on respectful and reciprocal relationships with the land and its rich diversity of peoples. She is honoured and grateful to serve as the Director of SFU's Research and Engagement Centre for Restorative Justice and on the board of North Shore Restorative Justice. Brenda believes that walking the talk in our own backyards brings justice home.

BRUCE MCARTHUR is an 87-year-old, retired construction worker who lives in a seniors' cooperative in West Vancouver, adjacent to the elementary school he attended in grade one. He has lived in West Vancouver for 68 years, most of that time in the Horseshoe Bay area. Bruce enjoys recollecting the past and sharing those memories with anyone who is interested.

CHANTAL CAMERON has called beautiful West Vancouver home for the past two years. Originally from Kamloops, she moved to the city over a decade ago and feels fortunate to live on the stunning West Coast. She works at the intersection of tech, data, and marketing, blending creativity with analytics. Outside of work, she enjoys travelling the world with her husband, spending quality time with friends, and prioritizing self-care through exercise and relaxation. Chantal is passionate about balancing a dynamic career with meaningful connections and personal wellbeing, drawing inspiration from new experiences and perspectives.

DR. DAINA ZHU is a researcher, ELL instructor, and mom to three lively kids. She's a devoted community champion for Chinese immigrants in West Vancouver, bridging language and cultural gaps with a warm smile. She'll try almost any cuisine – just don't ask her to bake (one scorching oven fiasco at a time). Need a multi-tasker? She's your pro, firing off emails, slurping noodles, and calling the plumber all at once. Dr. Zhu does it all, with humour and heart.

DEBRA DOLAN is a life-long private journal writer, pen pal, bibliophage, and a traveller who has sent postcards to herself since 1979. She is a member of the Story Circle Network, promoting women's stories internationally, and a self-described pluviophile. Debra enjoys intimate conversations over red wine, hockey, nature walks, solo piano recordings, and has completed two book projects: *Writings and Reflections: 1958 to 2018* and *Writings and*

Reflections: Turning 50 in 2008 (Walking the Camino de Santiago). Her work has appeared in numerous publications, including eight anthologies.

EVELYN (STEPHENS) DAWSON was a pioneer in business software development. Since retiring, she has developed a love of art, nature, and pets, especially cats. Through physical activity, she's become stronger and fitter on the path to regeneration. She also now has time to write about her life, which she enjoys, and to create vibrant colour combinations in her knitting. linkedin.com/in/evelyn-dawson/

HESTIA LI ANG has loved reading since the age of three, an interest that soon grew into a passion for writing. Hestia joined this program to connect with other writers and share her stories. With a deep interest in mythology and a love of multiple book series, Hestia is grateful for this opportunity and plans to participate again next year.

INGA PEDERSEN MCLAUGHLIN was raised in a small house near the mouth of West Vancouver's Cypress Creek. She fell in love with writing during Mrs. Guy's Hillside Secondary English classes. After a successful 12-year dance career which included Ringling Bros. Circus and the Moulin Rouge, she shifted to a career in stage management, working with Sir Andrew Lloyd Webber and

Disney. Her experience managing Broadway shows, national tours, and Olympic events worldwide has made her one of North America's most sought-after stage managers. She is always grateful to retreat to the peace of her Howe Sound home.

JENIFER DONG is kind and creative and has a passion for designing press-on nails, playing the piano, and enjoying the game *Dress to Impress* with her close friends. Jenifer maintains a YouTube account with a modest number of subscribers but is confident in her potential to become a renowned content creator in the future. Please subscribe to fancy_girl_jeni on YouTube. She would greatly appreciate your support.

JOHN WESTON, founder and Director of the Canadian Health and Fitness Institute (www.chfi.fit), has a diverse background in law, politics, business, diplomacy, and fitness advocacy. As an MP, he championed the Parliamentary Fitness Initiative and co-led the National Health and Fitness Day Act with Senator Nancy Greene Raine, inspiring 500 local governments to proclaim the day annually. At Pan Pacific Solutions Limited, John offers expertise in government relations, media, and communications. John and his wife Donna live in West Vancouver, receiving occasional visits from their peripatetic children, Shane, Jake, and Meimei.

KATE HUANG is currently a student at West Vancouver Secondary School. Her friends describe her as extroverted, energetic, caring, and funny. In her free time, she enjoys reading and snacking on Goldfish crackers and candy. You can ask her for advice but not to sing – it might get very loud! Kate has participated in many dance and debate competitions, and her favourite subject at school is English.

KIM KIOK WONG is an active grandmother who moved to West Vancouver seven years ago. She is a community builder and connector with Block Watch, Nextdoor, West Vancouver Foundation, Ambleside Butterfly Garden, and parkrun. She can be found walking the family dog, riding her bike, playing tennis or pickleball, or taking photos in her trademark yellow coat. Kim loves stepping out of her comfort zone to learn new things, like French, Spanish, and writing stories. She also enjoys sharing her beautiful city with visitors. Her favourite quote is, "Happiness is when what you say, what you think, and what you do are in harmony."

LAURISSE NOËL is grateful for the opportunity to contribute to this beautiful project. She lives on the North Shore and spends her time off walking near bodies of water and exploring places along the coast with those she loves and the sweet pups in her life.

LINDY HUGHES PFEIL collects rocks, loves the moon, and walks barefoot whenever she can. She believes *absolutely* that if we all sat around a fire and listened to each other's stories, we could bring about world peace. She facilitates writing workshops that break the rules, and her greatest thrill is witnessing people finding the magic in their stories. You can find her overfeeding the birds on her deck, traipsing along Marine Drive, or at LindyPfeil.com.

LORRAINE ZANDER is the founder of Faze Media (www.faze.ca), a lifestyle brand on a mission to support and empower young women and foster a mindset of empathy, kindness, and compassion. When she's not working on Faze, you'll likely find Lorraine on a squash court, or creating some edible art while cake decorating, or strolling along the Dundarave seawall taking in deep breaths of West Vancouver's mix of rejuvenating mountain air and ocean spray.

MAJA RUSINOWSKA lives in West Vancouver with her eight-year-old daughter, Scarlett. They enjoy walks along the seawall, relaxing at the beach, and visiting the local library. Proud to call West Vancouver home, they love hosting friends and family who come to visit.

MARIANNE PENGELLY is an artist, poet, and land steward.

MONICA HIGGINS admires animals across the size spectrum, from eagles to hummingbirds. She has learned how to be respectful of nature through taking part in the North Shore Eagle Network and exploring forests and coastlines.

PATRICIA L. MORRIS is an art school dropout and Harvard grad. When people speak about their identity, some include a dry sense of humour. But Patricia has a damp sense of death. (She lives in a rainforest.) Born in Winnipeg, she has lived and worked in places around the world – though not as many as her son and grandchildren. Ambleside's wet coast is her Ithaka, the notion of 'appropriation' expanded. She is not AI generated. linkedin.com/in/patricia-l-morris-6a11041/

SHIDEH KHORASHEH was born and raised in Iran until 1979 when she immigrated to Winnipeg, Manitoba. She has lived in Edmonton, Vancouver, and Stamford, Connecticut. She taught science and biology before pursuing her Master of Science degree and had a career in clinical research for 22 years. Now retired, she lives in West Vancouver, where she cares for her brother. She loves dogs, nature, art, gardens, travel, singing, and meeting people. She plans to write her memoir about resilience in the face of adversity.

VICTORIA KLASSEN is a writer, journalist, and communications professional from Ottawa, Ontario. She moved to Vancouver to complete a Master of Publishing at Simon Fraser University. As an avid skier, she is thrilled to be living near real mountains. Find her on Instagram at @TheCheerfulReader.

WENDY WILKINS WINSLOW has lived in West Vancouver all her life except for stints in Switzerland, Boston, Montreal, Saudi Arabia, and the United Arab Emirates. She adores her passel of children and grandchildren, who all live in the United States but know they're always welcome home if the political situation becomes untenable. This is Wendy's third contribution to the *West Vancouver Stories* series, and she is very grateful to Lindy Pfeil for her tireless support of writers.

YASMIN VEJS SIMSEK is an author, producer, and social justice activist, with an MA in Gender, Sexuality and Women's Studies from Simon Fraser University. She founded and now chairs the annual International Women's Day March Committee in Vancouver. Of Danish and Turkish heritage, Yasmin has published short stories, academic work, and a children's book titled *The Boy Who Was Always Warm,* the first of hopefully many focussing on representation of marginalised groups and family structures. She is currently also writing her first novel, and you can find her on IG @AuthorYasminVS.